The New Beyond Chocolate
Understanding Swiss Culture

Margaret Oertig-Davidson

Bergli

To my husband, Hans, my first teacher of
cultural values in Switzerland

ISBN 978-3-03869-070-2

First edition published as *Beyond Chocolate: understanding
Swiss culture*, copyright © 2002, 2011, 2015 Bergli Books.
ISBN 978-3-905252-21-7

Printed in Germany.

Also available as an ebook.

Bergli Books received a structural grant from the Swiss Ministry of
Culture, 2019–2020.

Contents

Introduction

"Learning to live in a new environment is in most cases a painful process of adapting to unstated rules and hidden differences."
Patrick L. Schmidt

I experienced my first cultural misunderstanding in Switzerland many years ago, during a three-week Interrail trip around Europe. I was a teacher of English in a residential language school in England at the time. Our adult students came from all over the world and stayed for three months. Many of them invited me to visit them, and so I travelled around Northern Europe, staying with various people, ending with a few days with Gabriela in Switzerland. She had said she would arrange a get-together with other ex-students from the school when I arrived.

Things did not go according to plan, and by the time I had travelled down from Norway to northern Germany, I was behind with my schedule. I phoned Gabriela on the Sunday to apologise and say I would be arriving a day late, on the Tuesday instead of the Monday, which was the next day.

When I arrived on the Tuesday evening I was met by Gabriela and two other ex-students and we had a drink together in someone's garden. I then discovered that they had arranged a surprise party with a barbecue for the Monday evening, to which around eight people would have come and brought food for the buffet. They were really disappointed that they had to cancel it.

I was very sorry about it, but was also quite puzzled that they had taken the risk of organising something that depended on everything turning out exactly as planned, such as trains running like clockwork on a long trip. Having grown up in Scotland, I did not expect trains to run on time, or even to run at all on some occasions. Having grown up in Switzerland, my ex-students were used to "trusting trains".

After over 30 years in Switzerland, I am now "Swiss" enough to find this incident a bit embarrassing. I would now do much more to try to avoid arriving somewhere a day later than arranged. At the same time, I am still "foreign" enough not to expect things to go according to plan. Attitudes to planning is one of the many topics addressed in this book.

Other cultural misunderstandings occurred in my first year in Switzerland when I decided it was time to get to know Swiss people better. I thought the best way to do this would be by inviting people I did not know well to our flat. Some people were clearly uncomfortable sitting in my living room. I was being "friendly", but they did not necessarily see me as a potential friend.

To my relief, when I then invited our Swiss neighbours for a Christmas drink and snacks, they were very pleased. They brought generous presents, and coped well with having to sit on the sofa, balancing their glasses and plates of food on their laps, without as much as a coffee table nearby. To my surprise, one friendly neighbour commented that he looked forward to coming again the next year. They saw it as my choice to open up my home to others and did not feel any obligation to reciprocate. Their relationships as neighbours usually ended at their front doors. This topic of expectations in relationships is an important one and is addressed in several chapters of the book.

In the early days, I also misinterpreted the approach of some of my husband's friends to making conversation. There was often what I experienced as an awkward silence as we sat around the table for a meal. I would "helpfully" start a new topic of conversation, as it seemed that no one else knew what to say. I ended up driving the topics of conversation and talking too much about myself, at least by Swiss standards. The topic of making conversation is also discussed in the book.

Reading an iceberg

If you are an incomer to Switzerland you may, like me, find that people are behaving in ways you don't expect or don't fully understand. Like me, you may be living with a local Swiss partner and are getting to know your partner's friends and relatives. (Around a third of marriages in Switzerland these days are binational.) Or you might be an expat working here, or an exchange student. Perhaps you don't even live in Switzerland, but visit regularly on holiday or on business, or work virtually from your home country with Swiss colleagues.

Trying to understand how the locals think in another country can be a bit like trying to read an iceberg. The tip is visible, but you still have to find out what exactly is going on under the surface. You will see little pieces of ice broken off and floating around on the surface of your daily life and interactions, available to be picked up and interpreted. This new edition of *Beyond Chocolate* will help you to make sense of the pieces and connect them with some of the underlying values and issues that are important in the local culture, but are not immediately apparent.

The locals
This book refers loosely to "the Swiss" and "the locals" for people who have grown up in Switzerland, or lived in Switzerland for a long time. They may or may not have a Swiss passport. There are officially 2 million foreigners in Switzerland. Four-hundred thousand of them were born here, but do not have a Swiss passport. The other 1.6 million are incomers.

It can be helpful to have people with more experience of local cultural values to explain what's going on. *The New Beyond Chocolate* introduces some of the cultural perspectives and intercultural experiences of incomers and local people around Switzerland. Most contributors live in the German-speaking part of the country, as I do, but there are also several stories and comments from Romandie and Ticino, the French and Italian-speaking parts.

The book is like a crash course in the wide and diverse range of Swiss ways of thinking and behaving. It explores unstated rules, offers insights into how people think and tells stories of how this impacts on the way they interact at work and in their private lives.

These are the types of stories you might hear at a social gathering, where different people give their personal perspectives. None of the views are "the truth," and some will be of more interest to you than others, depending on your own circumstances.

Book sections

Part One of the book addresses various aspects of being organised in your business and private life. I underestimated the importance of this topic when I first came to Switzerland. Part Two explores the question of how local people relate to each other and to incomers. In Part Three I discuss settling in to a new neighbourhood. Many tips are provided here. Part Four explores values in the Swiss workplace, with examples of cultural differences in the German, French and Italian speaking parts of Switzerland.[1] Project management, leadership styles and participative decision-making processes are all addressed, as are issues such as giving feedback and emotional expression.

In Part Five I address issues of relevance to students, covering topics such as interactions with lecturers, students and group work. Lastly, Part Six is specifically for people living in German-speaking Switzerland and focuses on the importance of High German and Swiss German dialect for integration.

I am very grateful to everyone who contributed their experience and insights to this book. Many of them have been given a pseudonym in order to remain anonymous. Some people have talked personally about difficult encounters and you may catch a hint of pain as they describe these. Having one's own value system challenged by the assumptions and values of others is at the heart of intercultural experiences all over the world, and adjustment usually involves discomfort in the beginning.

We all intend our experiences and opinions to provide a starting point for thinking about cultural values in Switzerland. It is my hope that the stories and insights shared will help you make the adjustment more smoothly, and that you will find a comfortable place on your own personal interface between cultures.

Part one: Being Organised

Chapter 1 Sticking to the plan

Perfect plans

Mara is a student from Basel who worked in an office in the USA for a few months. She got to know her boss's son, Justin, during her stay. He visited her the following summer when she was back in Switzerland, and met her friends. In mid-December, Justin contacted Mara on Facebook, saying, "I'm in France and am thinking about coming to Switzerland. What are you doing at New Year?" Mara wrote back, "Great. We're celebrating at my house with some friends. You're very welcome to join us." He replied, "Fantastic, looking forward to it." For Mara this was a definite arrangement. She then wrote to Justin shortly before New Year, "What time are you arriving? Do you need somewhere to stay?" To her surprise, he didn't reply. She didn't hear from him again until he wrote to her in February in a friendly manner, as if nothing had happened.

Making arrangements is an important topic that can affect everyone who interacts with the locals in Switzerland. For local Swiss people, keeping your word makes a good impression and is seen as a sign of depth and trustworthiness. Some people assume this must be changing and that young people will not mind if others don't keep to arrangements. Mara's surprise at not hearing from Justin again shows that this may not be the case. Even younger people may experience misunderstandings when interacting with visitors or incomers.

As the blogger Dimitri comments, "Many Swiss maintain a schedule for their social life. Even spontaneous happy hours are usually planned."[2] Mara was taking her invitation to Justin as seriously as she would a business appointment. He, in turn, was probably expressing an initial positive reaction to her suggestion at the moment of speaking, but did not see it as a commitment. The expression, "It seemed like a good idea at the time," is not used much in Switzerland. Tino, a Swiss-American, commented to me:

> When you see the amount of work which goes into a party in Switzerland, it's done much more professionally. The Swiss are likely to make perfect plans. People in the US don't know that. You have to communicate it somehow, and tell them more about what you're planning, so they realise how seriously you're taking it.

Making an offer is also seen as making a commitment by local people. Liam is a Swiss-British binational who was born in Switzerland to a Swiss father and British mother. When he was on business in the USA, he met his new co-worker, Nate. Liam discovered that Nate had never seen snow and said he would take him up a mountain to see some snow the next time he was in Switzerland. When Nate visited, Liam mentioned it again and Nate was surprised. "You remembered that!" he said. He had understood it at the time as a nice idea and had then forgotten all about it. Liam remembered it as a promise to be kept.

Pinning down the future

The way people talk about the future can be a cause of misunderstandings in intercultural settings. Everyone faces the human dilemma that we do not really know what will happen tomorrow.[3] Many local people in Switzerland use words to try to "pin down" the future and make it more certain. Once you have said you will do something, you have to do everything in your power to make it happen; otherwise you will be seen as an untrustworthy person. It is like a verbal contract, and sticking to it is a sign of a good character. The old-fashioned English expression "my word is my bond" reflects this concept. This has implications for employability, workplace projects, and deadlines.

In English-speaking cultures, your initial communication might just be a way to express ideas, wishes or intentions at the moment of speaking. Many people value an initial positive response to suggestions made by others, and take it hard if the other person immediately says, "No". Saying "Great idea!" does not commit you. Like Justin, you might just be brainstorming or exploring possibilities, with the assumption that you will confirm it later (known as "firming up" your plans) if you are sure you want to go ahead. Even if your plans are definite, you might see it as acceptable to change them at a later date. This was my naïve assumption many years ago when travelling by train from Norway to Switzerland (see the introduction to this book). Attitudes to planning is a key aspect of working internationally and more will be said about it in Chapter 15.

A Chinese client once told me that the lack of ongoing communication around arrangements in Switzerland was confusing to some Chinese people. In his view, if someone invited you to their home in China and didn't confirm it nearer the time, you could consider it cancelled. Not getting in touch any more would be a face-saving way for them to back out, if it didn't suit. For them it would be more comfortable if the local person took the initiative to contact *them* to chat a bit and firm up the arrangements, e.g. the exact time they would get together.

Invitations in Ticino

Carlo grew up in Basel but is often in Ticino, Italian-speaking Switzerland, as his parents now live there. He explains that it is hard to generalise for Ticino:

> Ticino is so small. Some people have only Ticinese families, but many have relatives in the German speaking part, and so have different experiences. Many young people study in the German or French speaking parts of Switzerland or in Italy – Padua or Rome. In general, although people are quite easy going, if someone says, "The next time you're here, come and see me", then they mean it. If they say, "The next time I come to Locarno, I'll give you a call," it's a commitment. It's similar in Italy.

Carlo explains that there are also many spontaneous invitations:

> It's very easy-going. I spend time in a village with 300 people, and one restaurant. So you go to people's homes. People say 'I'll cook tonight' . . . or even "right now" or they say, "Come for a drink." I also behave differently in the different environments. In Basel

it takes longer. It's a more formal invitation. We're not prepared mentally for a last-minute invitation.

Carlo also notices that Italian-speaking Swiss are less thrown by other people changing their plans.

Grammar lesson

The way language is used often provides clues to cultural attitudes. In English you can use at least five different verb forms to discuss the future. For example, if people are talking about whether they will be attending an event, they could answer "I will come, I am coming, I am going to come, I will be coming, I come." These five forms express different shades of meaning, although native speakers of English might not be able to explain why they use them.

English teachers explain to their students that "I'm coming" is used for an arrangement made with someone else. It sounds more definite than "I'll come." It can be called "the diary future". In contrast, "I'll be coming" sounds particularly definite and reassuring in English.

French and Italian speakers tend to report using only three of the six verb forms used in English. Most Swiss-German dialects have no future verbs forms at all. German-speaking Swiss learners of English don't have any use for six different ways to promise to do something in future. In Swiss German you just use the present simple tense and say, "I do it." Some English teachers call this "the future as a fact", like when you say, "Water boils at 100°" or "The train leaves at 5.22." It does not involve a human element, or should not, if it is a Swiss train. In Swiss German, if you are not 100% sure about something, you have to say "I might do it." As a linguist once said, "Grammar is thick with cultural meaning."[4]

Putting people on hold

"My word is my bond" sounds like a very old-fashioned attitude, but many Swiss young people put their trust in using words to pin down the future, as Mara's story shows. It costs them something to keep their word and it is therefore disappointing for them when others don't do the same. Flurina is Swiss and in her twenties. She told me how she went on holiday to Costa Rica with some Swiss friends. They found it stressful to make arrangements with people from other countries because they didn't stick to them:

> They would say they were going to the Sunset Bar at 7pm, and we would go home specially from the beach, get changed and then go along at 7 to have a drink with them and then they just weren't there. We think they kept their options open and changed their plan if something more exciting came along. It was very annoying but we got used to not really believing them.
>
> Some people in Switzerland weigh their options too, but they communicate it more clearly, for example, when you are arranging to go out together. Someone says, "Who's coming to the pub on Friday?" Most people will say, "Me!" or "I can't", or "I don't know if I can because . . ." but a few will just say vaguely, "I might come." You can't count on them, but at least you don't expect them. It's relatively clear.

Melanie Martinelli is a Swiss intercultural consultant based in India. She is the co-founder of The Learning Gym. I told her

Flurina's story and she wondered if the Swiss young people just hadn't waited long enough for their new friends.

> I go to a group class every week at my local gym in India. The first time I joined them they invited me to go the bar for a beer after the gym. I went home and showered, then went to the bar. I waited for an hour until they came. Fortunately, I had something to read with me. Some of them had bumped into other people or watched another class. I had assumed we would meet right after class.

What seemed to be an issue of keeping your word could actually be an attitude to punctuality. More will be said about this subject in the next chapter.

Workplace planning

When I first worked in Swiss companies in the 1990s, being described as "flexible" was not a compliment. It was considered much more important to be reliable, or trustworthy. It is hard to be both, as you can imagine from the examples above. *You* always do exactly what you have said you would do, but have to accept other people not doing so. Many local people in Switzerland manage to meet this challenge today, especially if they work internationally. Liam works as an event organiser in his international company. He explains that you have to plan differently for events in his company than in a traditional Swiss company, as his new administrative assistant found out:

> Our new Swiss admin had never worked for an international company before. She was panicking because 800 people had registered

for the Christmas party, and there was only enough space for 700. I told her, "Don't worry. Only 600 will turn up." She didn't believe me. A Swiss person assumes that almost everyone who registers will come. She would have believed me if I had said 30 might not turn up, because that many might have the flu. But I was right. She was quite shocked when only around 600 came on the night. As a rule of thumb, we say, "Count on up to 30% not showing up."

Swiss event planners in Liam's company also have to make allowances if people are flying in from around the world to attend a big meeting. They might have signed up for the opening dinner on the first night, but won't show because of jetlag or for some other reason. They will not necessarily see this commitment to come as written in stone. Who knows what the future holds? Things happen, plans change and they will not realise that people in Switzerland are counting on them 100%. Swiss employees tend to think in advance about whether they are likely to have jetlag, and if they might, they won't sign up for the dinner.

Gemma is English and works for the same company. She points out a difference if people are flying in to Switzerland from abroad and have signed up for events in their own team:

> You might have jetlag, but you feel more obliged. It is an opportunity to meet your team face to face. It is a smaller group and you will wonder why they are not there. Swiss team members are less likely to distinguish between the two situations. They feel they have to go to everything, even if they personally will not be missed.

Swiss people try not to make any false promises. This can make them sound a bit negative because they seem to be pouring cold water on other people's ideas and suggestions. The "cold water" is merely an honest assessment of what is actually possible as opposed to an initial positive reaction out of politeness to the person suggesting something. The subject of sounding positive or not in problem-solving situations is discussed in Chapter 16.

Cancelling everything

Paul works in a company in Basel and comments that it is not easy to ask people to change their appointments:

> Sometimes people's agendas are full of lunch appointments and meetings. They're inflexible, it's not negotiable. An English guy once sent us all an invitation and said, "Cancel everything you have." People said, "Arrogant bastard, telling us to cancel everything." But we wouldn't have been able to achieve what we wanted otherwise. Still, it's poor planning to send out an invitation to 20 people for the same week. If it is sent well in advance, for six weeks later, there's a reasonable chance it will work. If it is an urgent situation, it's more difficult.

The person telling everyone to cancel their appointments is seen as arrogant by local people in Switzerland, whereas to an outsider, the local people probably look a bit rigid and inflexible. Nathan suggests communicating actively to show the local people that the new event is important, while giving them the freedom to work out by themselves how to make it possible to attend at short notice:

> If I have to invite 20 people for a meeting or luncheon, I send the 20 invites but I know it might be difficult. I talk to them about it.

I say, "I'm expecting you. Can you just try to move something to make this happen?" Some get back to me and ask, "Should I move this or that?" I don't know and say, "Whatever is more important." In the end I leave it up to them.

The topic of changing tasks and appointments at short notice is discussed further in Chapter 15 on setting priorities.

Chapter 2 The race against time

Family subculture

When our children were small we lived in a suburb near Basel and often took the bus to town. The bus stop was quite near our house and there was a bus every 15 minutes. During the week, we were often running late because someone had lost a shoe, or needed to go to the toilet. At the weekend, when my Swiss husband was home, we never had to run for the bus. He would annoyingly remind us far too early that it was time to get ready, and spoil the fun of "the race against time". I only became aware of our family custom when Karen, a visitor from England, came for lunch. We decided to take the bus to town together and my four-year old daughter Fiona looked quizzically at Karen's elegant sandals and asked, "Can you run?"

Whether or not people are rushing at the last minute can be a matter of personality or upbringing (yes, my mother used to make us run for the bus), but I see a cultural component to it too. You just don't see many people taking the risk of cutting things fine and running for trams or buses in Switzerland. People will stare at you, which is slightly embarrassing, and in addition, they might think you're not organised, which can be seen as a bit of a character deficit. Enjoying the adrenalin kick of a rush of physical activity is reserved for hobbies such as river rafting, dirt bike riding or sky-diving, not catching a bus.

One of the reasons you can have high expectations regarding punctuality in Switzerland is because public transport tends to be very reliable. My 7.20 train is on time, trams have their own tracks and city buses have their own lanes. They tend not to get held up in traffic jams. We once had two students staying with us from Istanbul who were used to being caught up in heavy traffic there. They were attending workshops at my daughter's university and were intrigued that she saw it as possible to plan their arrival at the university the next morning for 9 am exactly.

(Reasonably) punctual

Young Swiss people are still reasonably punctual. Joshua is in his 20s and plays floorball. He says it is acceptable to be a bit late but if anyone is going to be later than 7.40, they message the team in WhatsApp and give a reason. Jana is Swiss and says she tries not to be more than three minutes late for a friend who is waiting out-side somewhere. "After four minutes I will message them to tell them, so that they can go into a shop or something. If we are invited to someone's house for 7 pm, and they are cooking, I will message them if I am going to be more than ten minutes late."

I asked Jana how it looks if you arrived at 7 on the dot. In Scot-land, people refer to this as being "a bit sharp". Don't you appear a bit obsessive? "No. It just means you looked up a tram and picked the right one," she replied. "But some people never get the tram right. If they are always half an hour late without an explanation, people get fed up with them."

Helping Swiss people to be late
If you have a Swiss partner, and are moving in international circles, you might need to train them to be "late" for some appointments. If my husband and I are invited to dinner at 7.30 pm by British people, I tell him we are invited for 7.40 so that we don't arrive any earlier than that. He knows it's not true, but goes along with it. In Britain people expect their hosts to be running late and to need more time than they had imagined. "7.30 for 8" is a handy way to arrange things in intercultural circles. This means you will start eating around 8, but can arrive any time after 7.30, as it suits.

Punctuality in Romandie

Marlène is French and Swiss and compares attitudes to punctuality in France and in Geneva, where she lives:

With my French friends, we often say we will meet in this bar at 8.00 and if we want to move somewhere else afterwards, we will see. Of course, nobody is on time. Some arrive at 8.15, others at 8.30 and some at 9pm or later. We are really free and not stressed by the time because we know we have all night to enjoy time together. In Switzerland, it's totally different. If you're not in the bar on time, they will harass you until you pick up the phone. They will then be a bit angry at your being late. They're much more preoccupied by time.

Loïc is from Lausanne, and agrees that French-speaking Swiss people will not be more than five minutes late when they meet in a restaurant. If they go to someone's house, they might be up to 30 minutes late. "People know their friends and their habits, so expect some people to be later than others," he told me. "It is polite to be 15 minutes late. This is known as "*le quart d'heure Vaudois.*" (In France people refer to "*le quart d'heure de politesse*", or the "quarter of an hour of politeness").

Claire is English and also lives in Canton Vaud. She comments that workmen always start and finish when they say they will and children are taught to be punctual at school. "There is no acceptable excuse for being late other than that the school bus is late." In contrast, she has a different experience of parents' meetings at school: "Events at school never start on time. They start ten to 20 minutes late, and people are still turning up after that. Everyone here's a bit flaky." It may be connected with having to organise childcare for their children in the evening.

Punctuality in Ticino

"In the Italian part of Switzerland it doesn't matter if I'm on time or not," said Carlo. "10 or 20 minutes late is okay too. It's not only a matter of personality. It is also the cultural environment." When he attended a conference organised by the local Ticinese government, it was intimate and easy going. Everything started 10 minutes later. "It makes a difference. In comparison, when I attended a conference I attended in Ticino organised by a national government ministry from Bern, everything started punctually." When it comes to visiting people in Ticino, Carlo sees it as totally acceptable not to arrive on time. "For people with children it's normal to be late, 10, 20, 30 minutes late for dinner," he explains. "Or even without children, up to 20 minutes is no problem. If people are later than 20 minutes they write a text or make a phone call and say, 'The kids are still sleeping' or 'We're stuck in traffic.'"

Workplace punctuality

Many international companies in Switzerland have flexitime, and people can arrive at work at a different time every day if they want to. Starting later also makes sense if you are working with different time zones. In traditional Swiss companies, people tend to start work early. Punctuality is still expected and good advance planning is a necessary skill. Some Swiss people will equate starting work later with laziness, even if the person concerned works the same number of hours as the early birds.

French influence
A study of a French company operating in several offices across Switzerland showed that the company culture at the Geneva office most resembled the company culture of the France-based headquarters, as many French nationals worked in Geneva. This could be seen in the starting times in the morning. They started earliest in Bern and Zurich, a bit later in Lausanne, and later again in Geneva.[5]

People tend to start work earlier in the country than in the cities. Perhaps the standard is set by local farmers, who need to get up early to milk the cows. Joshua is an engineer for a timber construction company in a village in Canton Bern. All 100 employees are expected to be at work by 7 am and Joshua's project planning meetings always take place at 7.30 am. I asked Joshua why being late is a problem. "If someone is late, then ten people are being kept waiting by one person," he explained. "That can't be. Time is money." I asked him what impression someone gives if they arrive late. "Someone who is regularly late won't work for us," he replied, "or at least not for long. It's a question of character. If he's late, he won't be precise in the way he works either."

Like keeping to arrangements, being punctual is a sign of reliability, or even trustworthiness. It shows respect for the other person or the group. In Joshua's company, your ability to be punctual is taken as an indication of your ability to work exactly. Employees are also aware of the bottom line, and keeping others waiting can be measured in terms of cost.

Impression management

In a study comparing French and French-speaking Swiss employees, it was found that arriving late for a meeting may infer different things in France and Romandie.[6] In France, the inference is that the person is working a lot, while in Switzerland when you arrive on time, you show that you are well organised. I once ran a series of workshops in a Basel company, and many incomers to Switzerland at a higher management level did not manage to attend or had to leave early. It came across that they were very busy people with other urgent matters. All of the Swiss managers attended and none of them left early. Their form of impression management meant that they showed that they were able to organise their time so that they could stay the whole day.

> **A hierarchical issue**
> From a Swiss perspective, you should be on time for everyone equally, no matter who they are. In some cultures, a higher status person has the right to keep lower status people waiting. Marcel is a Swiss teacher who worked in a school in Brazil. He had a meeting scheduled for 4 pm with the school's head teacher, who then didn't show up. He waited 20 minutes and then left. He was annoyed with her, but he discovered the next day that *he* was in trouble. She had arrived at 4.45 and had been annoyed that he wasn't there any more. She was his superior and a busy person with urgent matters to attend to. It was understandable that she could be held up. He was showing a lack of respect for her position by leaving. Local people in Switzerland would argue that it is a democratic attitude to give everyone the same degree of respect in meeting appointments, no matter their hierarchical level.

Loose and tight time

Melanie travels a lot between India and Switzerland. She talks about the concepts of tight time and loose time to describe Swiss and Indian attitudes to time.[7] In India lunch may lead to coffee, then to dinner:

> In India you have loose time. Times are not in your hands. If you're late, I'll use the time to do something else. It is seen as an

opportunity to network, chat to someone, make a phone call, read email, do anything. Or I'll rearrange my day and do B first, instead of A. Then you turn up and I say, "Give me five. I'm with B now." Everyone is used to waiting. A, B and C will all happen at some point. When you fix meetings and know there is going to be heavy traffic, you say to the person, "Give me a call when you're nearly there."

In Switzerland you have tight time. I have to plan more conservatively as it is seen as a failure if I don't meet my commitment. You win trust and recognition by sticking to what you said. In India, well you tried. That's okay if you don't manage to complete. The world is not predictable and you go with the flow. I now put in a buffer in my schedule in Switzerland. I say 2 hours even if I only need one. Then I can spend more time than planned on something.

Trustworthy job seekers

When I first arrived in Switzerland I assumed that my working and private lives were two quite separate worlds. I didn't realise that local people may expect similar behaviour in both. Jana is a manager in an international company in Switzerland and tells her friends about job openings there. She is quite careful about who she tells, as she explains:

If someone shows up late at the pub with no explanation, they come across as unreliable. I wouldn't want to hire them. Someone could have a great skills set but not be a good problem solver. At work you need to be able to deal with difficult situations where you have to find solutions to problems. Always being punctual shows that even if you run into difficulties, you can find ways to

Margaret Oertig-Davidson

anticipate and solve the problem. If the trams are not running on time, you get an Uber or cycle instead. You can't just say 'Damned public transport!'

I also wouldn't recommend Mara's friend Justin (*see last chapter*) for a job because I'd worry that he wouldn't answer an email or that he'd sound really keen and then wouldn't turn up to the interview. It's fatal if you can't make decisions and stick by them.

Jana may sound quite hard, but she is actually a very open and friendly manager. However, if she had been my neighbour, she would probably not have been impressed by the way I sprinted to the bus stop. It is worth doing a bit of impression management in this area and displaying your professional skills if you are looking for a job in Switzerland. You may know neighbours or the parents of your children's friends who can help you find a way in to the job market. If you show that you are trustworthy in your time keeping and in making arrangements, they are more likely to tell you about job openings they know about. This may be a more effective approach to job-seeking than attending official networking events with complete strangers. The topic of building relationships in the neighbourhood is discussed further in Chapter 6 on how people talk and Chapter 10 on getting to know your neighbours.

Chapter 3   Training in responsibility

Heads and legs

Thinking ahead is highly valued in Swiss everyday life, whether you are making plans, or catching a bus. In this chapter, I show how this is emphasised in the Swiss education system. David, a Swiss IT colleague, quoted a saying in German that he was taught during his apprenticeship: "Those who don't have heads have legs." He said this when he forgot to bring something to my office and had to go back for it. It can also be applied to lateness in the sense that if you don't plan well ahead, you might have to run instead.

I had unthinkingly taught my daughters about "cutting things fine", for example, running for the bus. Fortunately, they had their father and their Swiss school to provide alternative ways of going about things. This stood them in good stead in later years. The Swiss school system trains children to be well-organised and re-sponsible for themselves. I see the values taught at school as a key to how cultural differences develop.[8]

At the age of twelve, our daughter Fiona used to make a list for herself the night before she had a swimming class at school, because she needed to take so many things with her. She would then go through the list and put all the items in her bag. This saved her rushing around stressed in the morning, looking for things and facing a punishment for being late. I was impressed by it, because she thought it up herself. I had regularly forgotten things in those years when my teenage brain was a building site. I left books at home that I needed to take to school and vice versa.

Don't blame your mum

Fiona's approach was a two-stage process, first the thinking and writing, then the action. It had been part of her Swiss primary school education that she and she alone was responsible for getting organised. Explaining that your mum forgot to pack your home-work book, your pencil case or your money for the school trip does not wash with a Swiss teacher in any part of the country. It's your job to make sure everything is packed. There are real consequences and the equivalent of "black marks" if you slip up too often.

Lack of punctuality can have an impact on a job search. In many Swiss upper secondary schools (from age 15 to 19) they count how many times a year you are late, and put it on your report card, which is also your transcript of records, showing your marks for the whole year. An employer will then see this, as people include their final marks' lists in their job applications. It is like a reference.

It works perfectly

In Switzerland, being organised is a starting point for doing a good job, not an end in itself. The French psychologist and advertising consultant, Clotaire Rapaille, talks about the significance of qual-ity and perfection in different societies.[9] The Americans he asked associated the notion of quality with functionality. He concluded that the Culture Code for quality in American is "It Works." I would suggest that in Switzerland the Culture Code for quality might be "It Works Perfectly." Moving on to the subject of perfection, Rapaille found that it was experienced as something abstract, distant and maybe even undesirable in the US. He concluded that the Culture Code for perfection in America is "Death". It is not something we expect in this life. I would suggest that in Switzerland, having tools in perfect condition is seen as the prelude to starting work.

How the training pays off

A sense of personal responsibility is one of a set of key skills that are evaluated by Swiss teachers for the selection process to assess a child's suitability for a particular follow-on school. This typically takes place during the last two years of primary school around the ages of 10 to 11, and in some cantons, during the final year of lower-secondary school around the age of 14 to 15. There are three main types of criteria used. The first is marks from continual assessment, class tests and cantonal exams and the second is external exams. The third criteria type is centred round personal responsibility. It includes the teacher's all-round assessment of the pupil's attitude to learning and to school work. Being organised is a part of this.

Parents from abroad may focus on their child's academic progress at school and underestimate the importance of personal responsibility. It is, however, very important, whether pupils are entering apprenticeship programmes, a specialist school or gymnasium, – the academic stream of upper secondary school, which leads to traditional universities. The most demanding apprenticeships require really good organisational skills. Pupils and their parents have also commented on how mature a young person needs to be to manage gymnasium, which is educating young people for tough Swiss traditional universities.

In a report on gymnasium education,[10] pupils had to assess the importance of general study competencies and their personal competence level in each one. They assessed the following six competencies as most important: learning independently, working independently, taking responsibility for learning, time management, dealing with pressure, solving problems. In all of these, they assessed their own ability as lower than required, with a definite dip with regard to time management. They perhaps underestimated the value of their skills in getting things done at the last minute.

Part two: Getting on with the locals

Chapter 4 Relationships at work

Friends or colleagues

Shona came from Scotland to Switzerland with her children and
started a job as a team leader for an international company in
Basel. I spoke to her six months after she arrived, when she was
starting to be aware of differences in the way people were behaving around her. It was a bit like trying to "read an iceberg", as mentioned in the introduction. The differences were like little pieces
of ice broken off the iceberg, and floating around on the surface of
her daily interactions, available to be picked up and interpreted.
One of these pieces was the way the Swiss members of her team
referred to her:

> We all go for a social lunch once a week and regularly go for a
> beer after work but the only members of my team who would refer
> to me as a friend are the Englishman and the Swiss American. At
> various points in time I have heard the others refer to me as either
> their colleague or their "chief". I would refer to all of them as
> friends and colleagues. I have been finding it quite strange and
> mildly insulting.
>   The more subtle differences in culture only really become more
> apparent when you get the chance to draw breath, sit down and

start to take more notice of people and characters. In the beginning you are so overwhelmed with getting the fundamentals right, trying to pick up the language and trying to establish yourself in a new job that these are initially overlooked.

The way people speak can give an indication of how they think about their relationships. As Shona started to realise, the way her co-workers used (or did not use) words like "friend" can be an indication that things are different beneath the surface. Her story reminded me of how my daughter Fiona talked about her relationships when she was small. My children grew up bilingual, and sensed quite early that words were used in different ways in English and Swiss-German. One day, when Fiona was six, she started playing at the local playground with a girl she had never met before. They got on really well together. When it was time to go home, Fiona came rushing over to me and said excitedly, "I've made a new friend!"

It sounded like a comment made by a child in one of the British children's story books I read to her, and I was curious to know how she would express it in Swiss German. I asked her what she would tell her Swiss dad had happened. She answered in Swiss German, "*I ha öpper kenneglernt.*" ("I've got to know someone."). The budding relationship was the same, but she knew that the word "friend" wasn't used in Swiss German for someone you had just met.

The importance of lunch

A difference can be made between being friendly and being a friend. Stefan is Romanian and came from the Netherlands to work in an international company in Switzerland around ten years ago. One of the myths he had heard about Switzerland was that people wouldn't be friendly in the workplace. He did not experience this to be the case:

> In reality, people like to connect and network. They share stories and go for lunch together, although they may not invite you home. Coffees and lunches are a Swiss thing. They're very disciplined about organising lunch, planning it way in advance. In my team we all have different meetings, so we don't do coffee at a fixed time.
>
> Foreigners get used to doing this too. They see the benefit. There's less time after work, if you have kids, a family, but still want to connect to people. Lunch you need to get anyway. It's typically between 12 and 1. You're making a mistake if you go and get a sandwich and read the news at your computer.

Gate-crashing lunch
People are likely to schedule lunch with only one or two others they work closely with, have a lot in common with or want to build a relationship with. I once had a Dutch client who had started work in a small Swiss company. He went to the cafeteria on his own for lunch and when he had got his food, he went and sat with two colleagues he had spotted from his department. Their conversation suddenly seemed to dry up. With time he realised that he was gate-crashing and should only join people at lunch by invitation and started to set up his own lunch appointments. This idea of lunch being like a "private meeting" is not universal, but is worth watching out for.

The coffee break ritual

You can have a good social life in the workplace, as Stefan suggests. Networking is a good way to increase your visibility. "In big companies it's essential that you're connected to people, that they know you," said Stefan. "You know many, you connect better with some, and definitely want to keep in touch if they change roles."

It is important not to underestimate the importance of coffee break rituals as a way to get to know people. It might be tempting to see them as a waste of time, like lunch, and just sip your coffee at your desk, but they are the main socialising event in many Swiss workplaces. The time spent on coffee and lunches can add up to several hours a week of relationship building.

In big companies, where people interact with large numbers of colleagues, people often set up one-to-one coffee breaks with different people. In smaller companies and in clearly-defined teams, people may have a daily coffee break together at a fixed time for people of different hierarchical levels. Everyone is expected to come along. They are experts in finding neutral topics to talk about, like holidays, hobbies, sport and the news, rather than homing in on work or private issues that emphasise their differences. Anything that sounds boastful is also avoided. It can be a good idea to read a local or national newspaper online, so that you know what people are talking about.

Sitting at tables

"In Switzerland you sit in the coffee break at work like at a dinner table," Silvia said. "It's very formal. In the UK there are armchairs in the staff room. It makes for a different atmosphere." It is in fact unusual to sit together with people for any reason in Switzerland without having a table in front of you. If you go to people's homes for dinner, you may sit at the dinner table all evening. Perhaps this is why it doesn't matter that you take off your beautiful new boots in people's houses and eat dinner in your socks or the slippers they provide you. Nobody will see your feet anyway once you sit down. In the UK people are often keen to sink into the sofa and soft chairs for dessert and stay there for the rest of the evening.

Socialising outside of work

Stefan finds it understandable that work colleagues do not necessarily spend their free time together:

Connecting with someone privately is a time investment for everyone. If you're in your own country, you grew up there, you have friends there, you do not have so much interest in others. Isn't that the same everywhere? Some people in Switzerland may be reserved because they have said goodbye to too many people. They ask, "Why should I waste the energy?" Sometimes they do invest in someone settling here, and make friends, then the person from the other country leaves again on another assignment. The person who is permanent is disappointed. It wasn't meant to happen that way.

Although local people tend not to mix their work and private relationships, many are very invested in their work and share an important part of their lives with their work colleagues. They may find it just as enjoyable to talk to colleagues over lunch about their current project and company politics as to chat with friends over dinner about private matters. The relationships are just in separate categories, in different time frames.

As a team leader coming from the UK, Shona initiated going for a social lunch in a restaurant with her team once a week and an occasional beer after work. Stefan invites his team to lunch once a quarter:

> We used to go for a drink after work every two months, then I asked a couple of them what they would prefer. Some were drinking, but others just had a glass of water because they were driving. They said they would prefer lunch. So now we do lunch.

Going out for a drink together may be common among international employees, but there is no Swiss tradition of going out for a drink together on a regular basis. It tends to be a special event. Like Stefan's team, some people prefer to limit it to having lunch in a restaurant together so that they can head straight home in the evening. However, if you do invite colleagues to your home, they will appreciate it. You will be showing a high level of commitment to the relationship and it could bring benefits to the working culture in your team. Your colleagues may bring you generous presents as thanks, rather than returning the invitation.

Celebrating success

Chris is a Swiss project leader with team members both in the US and Switzerland. He told me about a "typical problem" whenever they want to celebrate a project success:

It is difficult to agree on what the team would like to do, and what would be appreciated by all. If you tell the people in Switzerland you are planning a party, half of them will say, "No, that weekend I'm doing something else," or "I'm spending time with my family." So it's very difficult. In the US, the Head of Development decides to have a celebration one Friday late afternoon because the team has had some good results. In the US everyone comes, and everyone says afterwards that they had a great time. In Switzerland, half of the people would just not come. They say, "We have work to do here, and if I now attend this celebration for two hours, then I have to work later in the evening to compensate."

Silvia is from Poland and worked in the UK before coming to Switzerland. "In the UK, if you are on a career path, you are expected to go for a drink with your boss at least once a week. Or play golf. I had a child and wanted to go straight home after work." At that time, Switzerland would have suited her better because there would be no obligation to socialise after work.

Melanie gives training courses all over the world. She finds it rare that someone will come up to her after a course in Switzerland and say, "Do you want to join us for a coffee?" If they do stay to speak to her, it is usually about the course. "They are task-oriented," she explains. "In the Arab world, Singapore or China people want to socialise with me and I never get a minute to myself." It has been my experience that Swiss course participants will have time to get together at the end of a course day only if they have planned it in advance.

As Stefan suggested, local work colleagues may not initiate going out for a drink with visitors or colleagues from other countries because they are not actually "in the market" for new friendships. They see it as something meaningful – as initiating a relationship – and do not want to "start something" or raise expectations. Younger people may speak English all day at work and be relieved to be able to speak their own language when they go out with their friends. If they are German-speaking, they may want to speak Swiss German together in their free time. More is said about this in Part 6 of this book, on Swiss German.

In their early days in Switzerland, many incomers arrange to get together at weekends with other colleagues from abroad who are also in the market for new friendships. These may also be the people they initially have the most in common with, experiencing the same settling-in process. In the longer term, work colleagues may also become friends. A well-chosen local neighbourhood may also turn out to be an excellent place to get to know people, as will be discussed in Chapter 10.

Chapter 5 Peaches and coconuts

Outer and inner layers

Before I settled in Switzerland, I moved around a lot, living in various places in the UK and Europe for only a year or two. I considered a friend to be anyone I would choose to have a coffee with in my free time. I heard other people from English-speaking countries categorise the people they got together with as "friends", "good friends", or "best friends". If you called someone a "colleague", it meant you worked with them but had no further contact. Calling someone an "acquaintance" seemed rather formal. It was like a deliberate choice, to distance yourself from them, almost like saying "he's no friend of mine". Talking about "someone I know" would sound more neutral.

A useful way to explain what words like "friend" can mean to people is the peaches and coconuts model.[11] This idea is thought to have been developed by German business consultants working with the USA.[12] They suggested that the outer layer of the peach and the coconut represent the public face of a person, and the inner layer represents their private life. The model is a simple starting point for thinking about a complex and multi-layered subject.

A peachy approach to relating to people is often found among people in English-speaking cultures who are fairly mobile, as I was. They make friends quickly, and see new people they meet as potential friends. It is easy to "get in" to the soft outer layer of the peach. People use first names, share personal information about themselves, ask others about themselves and quickly create a relaxed, positive atmosphere with each other. Deeper down, there is the peach stone and this represents the idea that relationships may not go deep. They don't have to, as they are not intended to be for life. In some cases they may indeed be deep and meaningful but for logistical reasons it is hard to maintain them long-term.

Meet my mum
Carol, an English manager working in Basel, told me that she got on very well with her Swiss assistant, Daniela. Daniela had even had lunch with Carol and her mother, when her mother was visiting Switzerland. In contrast, many Swiss people have never met their work colleagues' partners or other members of their family. They are unlikely to do so.

A coconut approach to relating can traditionally be found in cultures where people are less mobile, which generally fits for Switzerland. It involves making a clear distinction between people on the outside and the inside of the coconut. People with a coconut approach are not used to striking up friendships with "strangers" and maintain a respectful distance with acquaintances on the outside of the coconut. There is no sense of obligation to instantly create a friendly, relaxed atmosphere with others when they first meet. It takes time to warm up. (In fact, the idea of "breaking the ice" is a bit of a strange concept from a coconut perspective, as you just have very cold water beneath it. It is better to let the ice melt slowly and let the water warm up slowly too.) Because of the high value placed on independence, people who would be interested in getting to know you may respect your privacy and wait for you to signal that you want contact.

Sandbox friends

The inside of the coconut is reserved for people's long-lasting relationships with family and good friends, possibly people they have known since their schooldays. In Switzerland, these are sometimes referred to as their "sandbox friends". Many incomers comment that it takes longer to make friends with local people, but when you have a friend, you have a friend for life. People may invest a lot in these relationships, and maintaining them takes up a lot of their time and energy. They share more personally with each other and develop a deep commitment to each other for the long term. A friend is almost like a brother or sister. You know a person in quite a different way if you have been in and out of their house in childhood, getting to know their family too. There is a spontaneous intimacy at this stage of life, which is unlikely to be repeated.

Coconut meets peach
Theo has British parents and grew up in a Swiss village. When he was a student he studied abroad in Hong Kong for one semester. "I quickly got on very well with other British students and thought

we had developed a real friendship. But when I got back to Switzerland and wrote to them, they didn't answer." He realised that they had a peachy approach, while he had a coconut approach. He saw the initiated friendship as something long-term.

People who are not in this long-term "friend" category are often referred to as "colleagues", even if they do not work together. I used to think my Swiss brother-in-law had no friends because he only talked about his colleagues and good colleagues. Nowadays this may be masked on the surface by the all the "Facebook friends" people have, but in the non-virtual world, a friend is still a special category.

Commuting, not uprooting

An aspect of the coconut approach is the expectation that people will settle down locally after their apprenticeships or studies. Rosa is Mexican and commented that it is really important for the Swiss people she has met to stay in the same place as they have always lived in, and not go and work in another city or canton. "I'm now looking for a job nearby. All my friends here are from the same town too."

If people do find work in other cities, they often continue to live in the same place, and commute. They are not always willing to uproot themselves. Their long-standing friends are also their social capital in their community (see the box on page 52 for more on social capital). Their inside knowledge means they can help each other get things done, tell each other about jobs going in their workplace or help them find flats.

Statistics on commuting show that more people in Switzerland are continuing to live where they grew up and are travelling further to work than ever before. There was an increase in commuters from 2.9 million to 3.9 million between 1990 and 2016. Around 51% of commuters travel to another town to work and 20% to another canton.[13] Another trend is that universities are being built next to stations so that students can commute to university from their home towns. More is said about student life in Chapter 19.

Social capital
Social capital is a term used to describe the potential resources created by relationships of goodwill and trust. People have bonds with family and close friends and increase their social capital through building bridges or links to others. In Switzerland, people traditionally extend their social capital through their participation in groups and clubs, but may also develop loose ties by interacting casually with others they meet, like their neighbours. It might be that you enjoy a sport, and get to know people at the sports club, with whom you develop a relationship of give and take.

Swiss author Markus Freitag and his co-authors give examples of social capital in their fascinating book on the subject.[14] You might have the flu and a friend, kind neighbour or colleague will go shopping for you instead of you paying for an online grocery delivery. Or you helped a good colleague to move house last year and now it is their turn to help you carry your boxes. Or you and a friend both apply for the same job and the friend gets it. You both have the same qualifications and are both likeable people. However, he is a youth trainer in Swiss wrestling (also known colloquially as "breeches lifting") at the local club. Both sons of his future boss are active members of the youth section of the wrestling club. Social capital may lead to economic capital, but it may also remain something of emotional value that is not materially quantifiable.

Relaxed relationships

It could be argued that there are many people who take a peach approach in coconut cultures and vice versa. A peach approach could describe informal Swiss neighbourhoods or the local sports club mentioned above, where people are open to having relaxed relationships with a variety of new people.

Claire came from England to live with her family in Canton Vaud. It was an area where there were many incomers, Swiss and foreign, and she found people very friendly and welcoming. "My French is non-existent, so we speak English," she said. "The children my kids are friends with and their mums meet each Friday for a picnic lunch by the lake and have a chat." Claire also lives in a friendly neighbourhood. "Our kids know most of the other kids. There is a Halloween party and a Christmas party in the street and they invite everyone. Our kids get invited too, even though they are older than the other kids."

Some local people welcome the opportunity to practise their

English, and chatting with them in English can be an opportunity to get to know them better. This is a form of "social capital" that incomers can offer to local people from their first day in Switzerland. Its value in some circles should not be underestimated although, unfortunately, it can make learning the local language more difficult.

Join the club

The kind of opportunity to meet others described by Claire may not exist in more traditional, close-knit communities. Nathan also lives in Canton Vaud and comments that people where he lives are a lot more reserved towards foreigners coming through, like expatriates staying for one to three years. Incomers with permanent jobs usually find it easier to get to know the locals. If they have children, they are even more likely to find something in common. He recommends getting involved in local activities, which involves speaking the local language:

> The Swiss love it when you try to integrate and take on their culture. You find yourself doing things you never thought you'd do. I started skiing at 44 and now I'm an ice hockey referee. I've experienced getting to know a mixing of people from different walks of life in a way that would not happen in the UK. I go down to the local sailing club. This would be very prestigious in the UK. The billionaires at my club might have a ski chalet in Verbier, but they are mixing with council street workers. They all drive the same sort of cars. They don't care. If you see a Ferrari, it's usually driven by a foreigner.

Club members from different cantons

When my children were small I joined a local group of Swiss mums. I discovered after many years that only one of the women in the group actually came from the town we lived in. The others were "outsiders", from other cantons, but had married local men. By joining the structured group they could develop closer relationships over a period of years. I was the only one who didn't realise where the others came from. They all recognised each other's origins because of the regional dialects they spoke.

Members of a club may never visit each other in their homes, but will see each other more often than their long-standing friends. They also use first names as they do with friends. The importance of club rituals should not be underestimated, as Val, from England, describes:

> There are rituals that still hit me every time I turn up to the exercises at the local ski club. There are 60 people there and everyone shakes hands with everyone else, and greets them by first names before we start running around in a circle. It's quite hard because you're meant to know all the names. The same thing happens at the canoeing club.

Although it can be hard to remember sixty names, it is a good sign if you have an in-group of people to be on first name terms with. You may discover you "belong" to a greater degree than you had expected.

Chapter 6   How people talk

Talking personally

In my early days in Basel I often went shopping to buy things for our flat. I tried to chat to shop assistants to practise my German. While buying duvet covers and curtain material I told a shop assistant in conversation about the colours I was planning to do the bedroom in, and how my husband didn't think the colours mattered. She just answered briefly, along the lines of "Ah ja?" and over time I realised that it wasn't appropriate to talk personally to strangers, even if the topics were directly related to what I was buying. Curtains, yes, husbands, no. It was also noticeable that people in public places, e.g. out walking by the Rhine near our flat, did not expect to be engaged in conversation by people like me with whom they had not made an appointment.

Once I became aware of intercultural differences, I realised I had not only been talking to the wrong people, but I was also talking too much *about myself* (known in linguistic terms as self-promotion). Over the years I made the adjustment and got used to discussing more neutral topics in public places. A Swiss woman once told me that an American tourist started to tell her his life story

on a very brief trip across the Rhine on a ferry boat. She commented that she found it so superficial. I replied that for me, hearing
about a stranger's life is like reading a short story. You don't DO
anything with the information, and it doesn't lead to anything, but
it is interesting to hear it. Chance encounters can be enriching. I
enjoy taxi rides in English-speaking countries for the same reason.

Chatty border guards

It is a typical characteristic of people with a peachy communication style to talk to strangers as if they were friends. Emma is from
New Zealand and lives in Bern. She told me that the border guards
in New Zealand are really friendly when she goes back. "How are
you Emma? It's been a while since you've been back," they say,
glancing at her passport. They want to know what it's like in Switzerland. "Do you like it there?" they ask.

Sue, an American woman who had just arrived in Switzerland,
reported that it was easy to chat to locals when out walking her
dog, but they seemed to be taken aback if she ventured away
from the topic "dog", or asked them their names. It was probably
all going too fast for them. A degree of involvement has to be built
up over time. Pat is Welsh and has lived in Switzerland for several
years. She now really enjoys the relationships she has built up over
the years while out walking her dog. She jokingly calls the people
she chats to her *Hundeverein* (dog club). "Swiss people have a
sincerity but a distance, which suits my temperament. I meet some
other dog walkers again and again, and we talk about God and the
world."

In step with the locals

In the conversations she initiated, Sue was not in step with the locals and neither was I when I was buying curtain material. In Sue's case, it probably just needed a few months of meeting the same people while dog-walking for conversations to get going. In the case of people meeting in a shop on a one-off, there would be no relationship building up over time and local people would see the sharing of personal information as pointless.

In any interaction (and it may not only be verbal) we are negotiating the degree to which we are involving the other person or granting them independence (in everyday language known as "giving them space"). It depends on personality and gender as well as the type of culture we come from. Sue was quite an extrovert and wanted to involve people in conversations beyond dog topics, but being asked to give more information about themselves to a stranger may have made the other dog owner feel uncomfortable.

The Hong Kong based linguists Scollon and Scollon use the model of politeness strategies of involvement or independence to compare how people interact in the USA and Asian cultures respectively.[15] Strategies of independence tend to be used more in Switzerland with strangers than in western English-speaking cultures, both in business and in the local community. Some key features of these different politeness strategies are outlined below:

Politeness strategies of involvement
(often used in the outer layer of the peach)

* Smiling at strangers and chatting to strangers as if they were friends
* Using first names to break down barriers
* Creating a relaxed and friendly atmosphere, possibly telling jokes
* Giving information about yourself
* Assuming you know something about the other person
* Trying to find out what you have in common by asking questions
* Making them feel included

Politeness strategies of independence
(often used in the outer layer of the coconut)

* Valuing correct behaviour more than friendly behaviour as a sign of respect
* Using surnames to mark boundaries
* Observing rituals, like handshaking, to show respect
* Not assuming you know anything about others, and not trying to find out either
* Finding small talk superficial or false (they don't mean it)
* Using silence as a form of distancing from a topic

I once gave the same workshop weekly for around 18 weeks for a Swiss company with many native English-speaking managers.

If local people arrived first, they stood around, shaking hands with others as they arrived, and introduced themselves in Swiss German by their first names. Then they got chatting about where they worked and what they did. They all sat down just before the course starting time. If English speakers came in first, they would sit down somewhere and start talking about the weather, the traffic or the facilities to me and anyone else sitting there. The different politeness strategies were very evident. The Swiss attended to the formalities first and found out who the others were, while the English speakers chatted informally without even knowing each other's names. In both cases, they were breaking down barriers of some kind but they went about it in a different way.

No help needed

Local people usually need an explanation of the involvement strategy "assume you know something about others". They cannot imagine this. An example might be to say to someone, "I'm sure you must be tired now," or otherwise tell them how you think they might be feeling. In an English class, after I had introduced these politeness strategies we happened to be discussing the "polite" expression, "How can I help you?" which is sometimes used on the telephone. Ralf, who is German, identified the phrase as a typical strategy of involvement. He would think to himself, "I don't need you to help me."

When Melanie was visiting Switzerland after some years in India, she saw a man at the station looking around as if he was lost. "Do you need help?" she asked him. "You're not Swiss, are you?"

he answered. He had been living in Switzerland for three months and was not used to people offering him help.

Kissing on the fourth date
Dating is of course a situation where people around the world may use involvement strategies with strangers. Even here there may be differences in the initiation rituals. "Dating is different in Switzerland," Anne-Sophie told me. "When I went out to a club in the evening in Brazil, after talking to me for five minutes, a guy started kissing me. In Switzerland there is no movement the first few dates. My Swiss flatmate joked, "You don't touch your date the first three times you meet. You can kiss the fourth time. Not before.""

Professional behaviour

I used to enjoy flying out of Switzerland with British Airways because of the personal touch in the way they related to passengers. With time I saw this more from a Swiss perspective when a BA flight attendant asked a passenger what he wanted to drink. "Whisky with ice," said the man. "Sounds good to me," replied the attendant as he reached for the whisky bottle. The flight attendant was expressing something they had in common, that he shared an appreciation for whisky. A Swiss passenger may not see the point in finding something in common with people he meets in passing and will never see again.

The fact that fewer such personal comments are made by staff dealing with customers in German-speaking cultures means that

English speakers may be tempted to describe Swiss people as distant. It is usually only a matter of time until foreigners reinterpret the Swiss distance (if it is polite) as professionalism. The more personal comments made by English-speaking staff about their drink preferences may start to look inappropriate or even intrusive.

I sent Emma an early draft of this chapter on how people talk and she wrote back with a comment on how she has changed over the years in Switzerland:

> In the shop in New Zealand, people will ask me what's in my shopping bag. They really want to know. That, combined with the question, ". . . and what are you up to for the rest of the day?" recently had me kind of flummoxed. For sure, there is a kind of local throw away small talk way to answer that question without going into my whole itinerary for the day and holding up the queue behind me, but I don't know it anymore! Funnily enough, I feel a bit affronted by being asked, or forced to answer in front of people in a small crowded café or shop.
>
> I have come to appreciate more and more the relative anonymity you can experience in Switzerland. That personal freedom not to be disturbed that you write about. I wonder if it might also allow you to escape definition – and on some level even be a kind of platform for reinventing yourself. Even if it is just in a local shop or café, if no one is asking you questions about your plans or your bag. In the absence of being asked anything, you're free to go anywhere and be anyone.

Holidays and fusion cuisine

There are many situations in which people mix strategies of involvement and independence. This can be seen in local neighbourhoods.

Mike and Aline are Swiss and recently moved to a new neighbourhood. Mike runs his own company, offering IT services to industry. His company is growing and he is always on the lookout for new business. One day he went for a walk with Aline and their five-year-old son, Noah. They met Paul and Laura, who were out for a walk with their daughter, Mia, who goes to the same kindergarten as Noah. Mike had not met Paul before and chatted for quite a while to him about their recent holidays abroad and fusion cuisine. Meanwhile, Aline and Laura talked about children's birthday parties. It was a casual conversation but Mike was building his network. It could be that he and Paul would one day do business together.

Mike did not mention his company in the conversation with Paul. He stuck to general topics and focused on getting to know Paul. The topics were fairly neutral too. Mike did not mention the power struggles they were having at home trying to get Noah to go to bed at night, as people like me with a more "peachy" approach might do. In years to come, he would probably also not make jokes to the neighbours about Noah's messy bedroom or how he chatted online to his friends all evening instead of doing his homework. Noah might one day be looking for a job or an internship and while teenagers who spend too much time chatting on their phones in messy bedrooms may do an excellent job at work, it is not necessarily the first thing you want a Swiss neighbour-cum-potential-employer to think of when you mention your child's name.

In international circles, you might build your business network by doing your job well and staying in touch with people you meet through your work. In Switzerland, you can just as well join a tennis club or a political party and that may lead to a job or some business.

It is not necessary to "talk shop" there. If you love cooking, or are a gardening enthusiast, then others will be interested in what you have to say, and not feel threatened by you. An alternative is to let other people be the experts. Ask the locals about the town, good restaurants or places to go swimming, and which mountains to visit at the weekend. Being a good listener is important, as will be discussed further in Chapter 17.

Chapter 7   Ritual behaviour

Dancing on the phone

Greeting people and using their names correctly are important aspects of ritual behaviour in Switzerland, especially in the German-speaking part. This is particularly obvious when you make a phone call. It is a bit of a dance[16] and if no one teaches you how to do it, it can take about three years to develop basic competence and another three to be truly sophisticated. You might like to speed up the process a little by studying the dialogues below. They are shown here in English but it would be worth learning to do it in German.

You phone the doctor's and speak to her assistant. Foremost on your mind is that you need to make an appointment. You begin with this when the doctor's assistant (DA) picks up the phone.

Beginners level
(You handle it as you would in English)

DA: *Praxis Dr Keller*, Gysin.
You: I'd like to make an appointment with Dr Keller.
DA: *Gruezi*. What's your name please?

You have two left feet in the telephone dance.

Intermediate level
(Basic competence).

DA: *Praxis Dr Keller*, Gysin.
You: *Gruezi*. My name is Catherine Shultis. I'd like to make an appointment with Dr Keller. (While you are saying 'I'd like to make an appointment with Dr Keller', you are drowning out the doctor's assistant, who is saying, *Gruezi, Frau Shultis*).

You're still a bit out of step in the telephone dance. You didn't say her name, or give her time to greet you.

Advanced level
(Sophisticated phone user)

DA: *Praxis Dr Keller*, Gysin.
You: *Gruezi, Frau Gysin*. This is Shultis. (Then you wait.)
DA: *Gruezi, Frau Shultis*.
You: I'd like to make an appointment with Dr Keller.
DA. So. . . .

At last, you are dancing in step. The steps are as follows:

1. They give their name.
2. You greet them by name.
3. You give your name.
4. They greet you by name.
5. You tell them why you're phoning.

It is not a great crime if you do step five before they get the chance to do step four, but many English speakers report that just when they are patting themselves on the back for having finally mastered it, they trip up again.

The dancing lesson could go on with reference to finishing the conversation – using names again and possibly wishing each other a nice day, evening, weekend, or Sunday. In German if someone wishes you a nice something in German, you can reply *"Danke, gleichfalls"* ("Thanks, same to you").

Other telephone tips

In German-speaking Switzerland, if you are phoning Lorenz at home and his partner Peter answers the phone, tell him who's calling and have a few words with him too. Don't hang up when he says, *"Tschüss"* or "Bye". He is just going to get Lorenz for you. Saying goodbye to you is a dance step too.

Peter may come back and say, *"Bist du noch da?"* ("Are you still there?") Resist the temptation to reply "No". He doesn't really think you've gone away, it's just the Swiss way to make contact again, the way English speakers say, "Hello?" when they come back to the phone. In French they say, *"Ne quittez pas"* ("Don't go away"), the way English speakers say, "Just a moment, please."

Categorising your relationships

It used to be easy to identify whether Swiss people were close to each other or not by their ritual use of names. They would use surnames with people on the outside of the coconut – neighbours, acquaintances and most people at work, and first names with people on the inside of the coconut – their families, friends and everyone they knew from their schooldays. They would change to first names if they had a good reason, like working in the same team. When they joined a club, a choir or a language class, they would use first names to express their belonging to the group, as they still do today. Nowadays young people tend to use first names with each other, and colleagues, neighbours and casual acquaintances may quickly change to first names too.

In German-speaking Switzerland, using surnames goes together with saying *Sie*, the formal word for "you" in German and using first names goes with the informal *du*. The type of relationship you have with people has an impact on the way you greet them, at least in the local languages. If you see Ramona Eng, a neighbour, walking towards you in the street, you need to get your brain in gear as you categorise the relationship. If you use surnames with her, you say, *"Grüezi, Frau Eng"* in German and if you use first names with her, you might say *"Hoi, Ramona"*, or *"Sali, Ramona"*. So even if all you wanted to do was walk down your street to the Coop to buy some milk, you will find yourself in a live sociological study, as you are dividing the people you meet on the way into "first name" and "surname" people.

This distinction is quite complicated for children, and in the 1990s, Swiss parents started to encourage them to just say *"Hallo"* to everyone they met, without using the person's name at all. *Hallo* is now often used by children, younger adults and foreigners.

Hallo, hallo

Two of my students from Germany told me about the friendly staff they had met in a Swiss supermarket. They went to buy some beer and Christoph put his pullover down on a shelf while he was looking at the different brands on offer. He and Manuel then walked on to the checkout. A member of staff kept following them and calling out to them, *"Hallo! Hallo!"*

"Hallo", they replied with a wave and a smile, and continued to walk. "Friendly people here," said Manuel. At the checkout the assistant caught up with them and handed Christoph his pullover. She had been using *Hallo* the old-fashioned way, not to greet them, but to stop them in their tracks and get their attention.

Use of names in Romandie and Ticino

It is not so important to say people's names in French and Italian. In French you can just say, *"Bonjour"* or *"Salut"* respectively and in Italian, *"Buon giorno"* or *"Ciao"*. *Salve* is a neutral option in Italian, although this may vary from region to region. The formal word for "you" is *vous* in French and *lei* in Italian. However, people may use the formal *vous* or *lei* and use first names. (German-speaking Swiss are not used to doing this.) The informal word for "you" is *tu* in French and *tu* in Italian.

Louise is a South African nurse and comments that in her hospital in Romandie, colleagues are using *tu* much more, even between doctors and nurses. "Young doctors say, *'tu'* to me so that they can ask me for a favour." Louise also experienced a senior doctor changing back to *vous* when he became a director of the hospital, which I had not heard of before.

Alessandro is a manager from Ticino, who is based in Zurich. He did not experience the use of *tu* instead of *lei* as very popular there:

> We were an English-speaking company in Ticino so we used first names in English, which didn't fit with the regional culture. People said, *"Buon giorno, Alessandro"* but used *lei*. They are very deferential. Changing to first names and *tu* over a glass of wine doesn't work there. They are my subordinates.

Compulsory greetings

"You can't just walk in to a shop and ask for something in Switzerland," Louise told me. "You have to say *Bonjour* first." I have also experienced it as really important to say a greeting before you start talking to people. I once walked up to a bus driver standing beside a bus, and said politely in German, 'Excuse me, does this bus go to the airport?' '*Grüezi,*'" he replied. For him, 'Excuse me' was not polite enough. I needed to say the greeting. After a pregnant pause to let the lesson sink in, he did go on to tell me that his bus went to the airport.

Loïc finds it funny that in Basel that he has to remember the names of people he is introduced to and then use their names when he says goodbye. In Lausanne you can just say "*Au revoir*" without demonstrating that you remember the person's name.

Like eating with your hands

Use of names is usually reciprocal in Switzerland, as an expression of degree of distance or closeness. You cannot have one person closer than the other. In English-speaking countries you may use your doctor's surname and say, "Dr Smith", while they just call you "John" or "Anne". That would be considered a lack of respect for patients in Switzerland. Teachers, too, make a point of using surnames names with parents, and if they use first names, it is because they know parents personally from somewhere other than the school.

Incomers usually use the surnames of doctors but may not think to do so with lawyers. Ursula is a Swiss lawyer who has worked with many foreign clients over the years. She and her colleagues are sometimes surprised by clients from English-speaking countries who write to them using their first names. Ursula is not even on first names terms with some lawyer colleagues from other firms. "It is as if someone was saying to us: "We do not need to use forks and knives, we are just eating with our hands today," she told me. Young lawyers use first names more widely and accept that it is part and parcel of speaking English with clients.

Insiders and outsiders

Traditional Swiss companies are introducing the use of first names as part of the company culture. The national Swiss rail company, SBB, now encourages all employees to use the more informal *du/tu/tu* and first names with each other throughout Switzerland.[17]

A clear distinction is still made between insiders and outsiders in the company. Employees will continue to use surnames with customers, partners, suppliers and candidates at job interviews. They will only "offer" first names once they have hired them.

If you start a new job in a traditional Swiss company, the etiquette is to use surnames with your colleagues until someone suggests changing to first names. Joshua in Canton Bern explained that he started using the *du* form with his colleagues on the same level from the first day of his job, at their suggestion. After around two months his boss also suggested changing to *du*. "If you work with someone a lot, the higher level person usually suggests it."

Kissing friends and family

When local people and incomers get together privately, in all parts of the country, some may "air kiss" each other on the cheek three times, instead of shaking hands. Some young people just kiss their good friends once, and in German and Italian-speaking Switzerland, some people now hug instead, or hug and kiss once. You need to have your eyes open to spot the latest fashion. Are they moving their head towards you or only stretching out their hand? Men do not generally kiss other men and some men do not kiss anyone if they can help it. In my husband's extended family, my husband, one brother and one sister-in-law shake hands with everyone, while everyone else kisses. It can be quite confusing to know whether the people you are with all want to do the same thing.

Louise describes how she tries to simplify the ritual. "A lot of people kiss everyone in the room when they leave, even if they've just popped in for ten minutes to say "hello". I try to escape with a general "goodbye" and a wave into the room, so that I don't have to do the round of kissing twice in ten minutes. They call this *partir comme un anglais* (leaving like an Englishman) which means you are leaving without saying goodbye.

Kissing at work

Shaking hands is the safest option at work until you can figure out what other people are doing. Moving on to kissing colleagues is a bit more common in Romandie than German-speaking Switzerland. Chantal is French and told me that in Lausanne, if she knows colleagues well, she kisses them three times. "When they come to Lucerne, my reflex is to shake hands with them. Then they say, *'on fait la bise'* so we kiss. It brings some warmth into our working relationship." Louise mainly sees young people kissing at work in Romandie if they are friends as well as colleagues and haven't seen each other for a while.

In international companies, you might see handshakes, kissing or even hugs. Lisa comments that people used to shake hands in her American company in Canton Vaud, and then they stopped that and started just saying "hello". "But Germans would prefer a handshake," she said.

It gets more complicated if people are shaking hands with some colleagues but kissing or hugging other colleagues they know well. Elenor is Swedish and works in Basel. She told me about hugging her female Canadian boss. They get on very well and they hadn't seen each other for a while. A new higher-level boss from the USA was visiting and was just being introduced to them. He thought the hug was the local custom so he hugged them both too. He was then embarrassed when other female team members arrived and shook hands with him and each other. His live study was based on observing too few people. I can see why they decided just to say "Hello" and not touch at Lisa's company.

Rituals around food and drink

Another ritual worth observing is the idea of waiting till everyone is ready before you start to eat or drink. Richard, an American, was once out for lunch with his colleagues in a self-service restaurant. He and his colleague Irene were in a hurry because they had a meeting afterwards. Everyone sat down at the table with their food, except for one person, who got held up. Richard started to eat but noticed that Irene waited with the others until the last person had sat down at the table. Then they all said "*n Guete*" (enjoy your meal) and started to eat. In French you say "*Bon appetit*" and in Italian "*Buon appetito*" for "enjoy your meal".

If people are having a glass of wine together, everyone raises their glasses at the same time, says "cheers" and looks round at everyone else before they take a sip. Many groups will also clink glasses with everyone individually, before starting to drink. This may involve getting out of your seat to reach everyone. It is important to look into their eyes, and say the equivalent of "Cheers" and their name as you clink glasses. This is a bit tricky as you also want to look at their glass to make sure you "hit" it. Some local people are really into making sure the edge of the glasses clink together, as this makes a nice sound. I used to just bash the side of people's glasses, and thought it was a good start.

In German, people may say "*Prost*", "*Zum Wohl*" or even "*Gesundheit*" while in French they say "*Santé*" and in Italian, "*Salute*" or "*Cin cin*". Taking a slug before the others are ready means you are out of sync. If you are in a mixed nationality group, you may be eating your dinner, still waiting for the host or the boss to initiate the glass clicking ritual and suddenly notice the others have already downed half of their glass.

If you are milling around at a stand-up drinks party with snacks (often called an *Apéro, apéritif* or *aperitivo*), you can clink glasses individually with people as you come across them. This is often the most dynamic phase of an *Apéro* as people do the rounds, before they come to a standstill and chat in pairs or small groups for longer. It can be quite hard to break into these conversations so it is good to arrive early if you want to speak to a wide variety of people.

Chapter 8   Taking up space

Negotiating shared space

How much space we occupy, both physically and psychologically, is an important topic in Switzerland. In this chapter I explore the topic in our everyday lives and in Chapter 17 it is discussed in relation to workplace communication.

When you land at a Swiss airport and walk through to the luggage carousels, you may notice that there are few advertisements and the ones you see usually have a lot of white space. Leaving lots of white space on the page in advertisements conveys an impression of an upmarket product. Not all space has to be filled. It can be tasteful to leave some empty.

With regard to our behaviour, in our everyday interactions we are making decisions about space all the time. How much space can we take up without making the people around us feel we are "in their faces" or intruding on their personal space? The fact that some space is empty does not mean it has to be filled, as many of us find out the hard way. People are expected not to regularly leave things lying around in shared space, like their bicycles at the communal entrance to their block of flats, or their children's toys in the sand box of the communal garden. Neighbours live close together and have to learn to negotiate all of these issues. They value their free-dom, but put the emphasis on freedom from being disturbed by others rather than the freedom to do as they please.

As well as the use of physical space, Swiss people are aware of the issue of "auditory space" that is shared, even if I have never heard them call it that. A classic bye-law is that people should be quiet in neighbourhoods between 10pm and 6am on weekdays. There are allocated times to make an excessive amount of noise, such as for the carnival or a summer festival. My brother and his family were visiting us from Scotland recently and took great care not to make any noise on our balcony after 10pm. They were then speechless on the Friday evening when a rock concert started in a nearby park around 10pm and went on until well after midnight. The same thing happened on the Saturday.

I had to explain that the organisers would have obtained permis-sion from the authorities to make a significant amount of noise for two evenings in a row. More is said about negotiating expectations related to noise in Chapter 11 about conflict with neighbours.

Ranting at the bus driver

It is of course an option not to follow the norms. Emma from New Zealand describes herself as anti-authoritarian and anti-establishment:

I used to enjoy snubbing my nose at the rules – ranting and rav-ing at buses pulling away from the stop, while I stood knocking on the door, shouting, "I was just here!" I ended up yelling in English if I got angry. I am now finding myself able to shut down my impulse to rant and rave at the bus driving off. It's not what we do here.

People are concerned about disturbing others while travelling and will also insist on their own right not to be disturbed. While I was writing this chapter I overheard a mother of two young boys telling them on the tram, "I don't know if everyone likes it much if you talk so loudly." She was making them aware of the impact on the people around them rather than the fact that it bothered her. I was once in the silent compartment of a train where two English speaking tourists were chatting quietly to each other. A man typing on his laptop pointed out to them that it was a silent compartment and that he was working. They were very surprised. They probably imagined talking in low voices was quiet enough.

Women laughing loudly

Laughing too loudly can be an auditory space issue too. In their early teens, both my daughters told me that I laughed too loudly – for a mother. It was highly embarrassing for them. One of them complained that when I laughed at the checkout in the Coop super-market, people could hear me away at the back of the shop. (She was at that age when it was also embarrassing to be seen with me wearing my woolly hat in minus temperatures – and listening to my bad Swiss German was very painful for her indeed.)

Apparently, Swiss mothers did not laugh as loudly as I did. My younger daughter demonstrated "laughing like Swiss mothers" for me. This involved twisting my head down to the right and giggling quietly into my right shoulder. I started to use laugh-ing loudly as a threat when my daughters were not doing what I wanted. I recently mentioned the laughing issue to my daughter's friend who said that her Dutch mother also laughs very loudly. Her Swiss father apparently laughs loudly too, but that is normal for men.

With time I discovered that laughing loudly was a power issue. I was told by participants in a course for office assistants that secretaries should not laugh louder than their bosses. So if you are a a foreign woman with a loud laugh, and you go for a job interview in Switzerland, you might like to try giggling into your shoulder like a Swiss mother at the interview and reserve your belly laugh for once your three-month trial period is over and they really value you for your skills.

Assaulted by smells

How people smell may be a bit of a surprising "olfactory space" issue, but people sometimes complain about being assaulted by other people's strong perfume or aftershave on the tram or in restaurants. I certainly notice young people wearing more perfume or aftershave in the UK than in Switzerland and Swiss deodorants tend to be less scented than British ones.

There is one smell you are allowed to assault people with in Switzerland, and that is the smell of strong cheese. You can keep it in your fridge, and serve it to guests for dinner in a fondue or as raclette, poured over potatoes. I remember the newspaper reporting a funny incident during the European football championship in Basel several years ago. There were many Dutch fans milling around in Basel before their matches and some local Basel fans dressed in orange too, to show solidarity with the Dutch. A Swiss man dressed in orange was standing next to a stand selling Raclette cheese with potatoes. A Dutch man walked up him to talk to him. "I'm not Dutch," the Swiss man told the Dutch man. "I know that," replied the Dutch man. "If you were Dutch, you wouldn't be standing so close to this smelly cheese stand."

One thing you *can* do more of in Switzerland without being considered intrusive is to *look* a lot, for example look strangers in the eye in public places. My Swiss brother-in-law explains that when he does this, he is not staring; he is just "checking", as a kind of social control to make sure he knows who is there and that everything is all right. (It is happening less these days because people are busy looking at cute kittens on their mobile phones when sitting on a tram or train.) Swiss driving instructors even tell you to look people in the eye at a crossroads to make sure you are in agreement as to who has right of way. In many cultures this is considered provocative, or aggressive. I have seen web sites abroad that recommend that you do not look other drivers in the eye in order to avoid road rage.[18] Fortunately, in Switzerland you are unlikely to get punched for eyeballing people, laughing too loudly, talking on your mobile, or smelling too strongly.

Getting above yourself

The way you present yourself is also a psychological space issue. The Swiss media are hard on people who draw attention to themselves. Dirk Schütz, editor-in-chief of the Swiss business magazine, *Bilanz*, describes the practice of using a middle initial, such as Donald J Trump, as a terrible custom. Name expert Marc Hauser advises Swiss managers not to join in such "letter games". "They actually want to appear important – and this intention is recognised immediately if someone suddenly insists on a middle initial."[19] If you have to do something where you take centre stage, like Roger Federer playing tennis, it is important to do it with a suitably modest manner.

Even medical doctors should not get above themselves. In the Genevan newspaper *Le Temps*, etiquette expert Silviane Roche explains that she will ask for "Doctor So-and-so" on the phone, but will then address the doctor directly as "*Monsieur*" or "*Madame*", without using the word "Doctor".[20] She never has the feeling they would be hurt (*blessé*) by this. She would find it very stiff to say "Doctor", especially as she is increasingly old enough to be their mother. She explains it by saying there is a tendency towards abolishing formalism. Similarly, it is fine to just say "*Herr*" or "*Frau*" or "*Monsieur*" or "*Madame*" to people with PhDs in Switzerland. They should not want to appear more important than others without titles. "Switzerland understands itself as a confederation of equals" explains columnist Philipp Tingler.[21]

Looking lazy

Many space issues are related to a broader topic of sensitivity regarding how things sound or look to others. I recently discovered that Hans, my Swiss husband of over 30 years, doesn't like me wearing my dressing gown long after I have got up. "It confuses me if you're in your dressing gown at 10 or 11 in the morning," he admitted. "I know you might have been working for hours at the computer. But in my mind it has a connection with laziness." I wore my dressing gown to work at the computer because I was so deeply engrossed in what I was writing that I could not drag myself away to do anything else, not even to shower or get dressed.

I remembered that when we visited Hans' mother, she had sometimes worn a tracksuit in the morning before she went into the shower. In fact, she bought me a tracksuit once and told me it is really useful for when you get up if you don't want to get dressed yet. Then you can still put your rubbish bag out on the street or collect your letters from the letter box outside. I got the message then that I should not be seen outside in my dressing gown. I realise now that she had possibly thought I should not be seen in it inside either.

I discovered that a dressing gown is the right gear for specific situations. I was out shopping recently with my Scottish friend Megan, and she pounced on some white bathrobes with a waffle pattern in a Swiss department store. "This is what I need!" she said. She had just moved in to a smart new Swiss flat with a swimming pool in the basement and needed a new dressing gown to "look the part" when she goes swimming after work. "My flowery dressing gown is too colourful," she explained. "The neighbours in my old block of flats used to stare at me when I wore it to go down in the lift to get my letters." Her new white dressing gown looks like the ones guests are given in hotels with swimming pools to wear to walk from their bedroom to the pool. It looks more purposeful, even sporty. Like the tracksuit.

Part three: Meet the neighbours

Chapter 9 A good place to live

Finding a good place to live is not just a matter of choosing the best house or flat for your needs. It is also worth thinking about where you will feel comfortable, whether you want peace and privacy or the opportunity to make friends. Neighbourhoods can vary greatly, and it is worth comparing settings or getting a recommendation to find one that will suit your situation, or where other people live that you already know. If you have children, you might like to find a place where there are plenty of other young families around.

Tanya is from the USA and has lived in Basel with her family for many years. She described the contrasts she experienced in the different neighbourhoods she has lived in:

First we lived in an apartment surrounded by mostly older neighbours, and we had very little contact. In our second apartment they were also older, but this time we took the initiative to invite them over, like for an *Apéro* after our baby's birth, and got to know them better. Finally, we moved into a townhouse on the other end of the first street we had lived on ten years before. By this time a lot of young families had moved in alongside the older people (it was about half / half) and we were surprised at how outgoing and friendly they were. People came up to us and said. "We're glad you've moved in!" and when my husband went out to do a bit of gardening, at least five people stopped to talk to him. Some invited us over for drinks.

Several neighbours let me know that there were some lovely activities for young children at the local church as well as annual family events such as meeting *Santiklaus* (Saint Nicolas) and a movie night at the local park. Many of the neighbours put up Christmas lights on the same day and made a "happening" out of it. Groups of children have even started spontaneous trick-or-treating on Halloween.

Our neighbours appear to be open to old and new traditions, but most importantly, they are interested in positive contact with each other. In general, I would say "new" people take more initiative to make contact than older residents. In this neighbourhood, the younger generation is creating a peach culture. On the other hand, we have very fond memories of our previous neighbours once we got to know them.

This example shows how difficult it is to generalise about what your relationships in a neighbourhood could be like, even within the same Swiss town. It is not only a question of how friendly you are, as Tanya knew. She mentioned age and the influx of new people moving into the street as factors affecting how much contact people make.

Thinking local

If you work in an international environment in Switzerland it is not immediately obvious that community life in Switzerland can be very parochial. Swiss colleagues in global companies may seem very cosmopolitan but in their private lives they still tend to think local. Even though a Swiss business person may regularly be travelling to New York and Paris on business, their family might have all their schooling, classes and clubs within a couple of kilometres of their house and walk or cycle everywhere. Even in larger towns with less close-knit communities than small villages, people may still operate within the immediate neighbourhood as if breaking down the town into more manageable units.

Most communities try to provide a kindergarten and school in the neighbourhood so that children can walk there unaccompanied. Parents also prefer not to have to go far to take their children to their after-school classes. They do not want to offer an *Elterntaxi* or "parent taxi" service. Mothers who drive their children across the city to the best dancing class in the region are considered to be stressing their children and living a very stressful life themselves.

Moving to the country

Given the very localised thinking, in what kind of a community are you likely to feel at home in Switzerland? Stephan is a Swiss father of young children, whose job involves working with small villages. Generally speaking, he finds it much better to live in a village than in the city, because of the beautiful countryside, and the high quality of life. It can also be an advantage that you will get to know the neighbours fairly quickly. However, for foreigners, he would only recommend villages that are open to change:

In some villages in Switzerland a hundred new houses are built every year, and well-heeled highly-qualified people move in, who work in the city. The inhabitants are more open towards another culture. A way to know if a village is like this is to see how many new houses have been built recently and how many newcomers have been settling in the village over the last few years. It is a very positive indicator if a village organises a *Mittagstisch* (organised lunch for school children). This shows openness to the idea that both parents can work outside the home. In a village I know, the men will say "We don't want a *Mittagstisch*. I want my son to be able to come home for lunch."

It is Stephan's opinion that in villages with up to 2000 inhabitants it is a tradition that everyone knows exactly where everyone else is at any given time. (You could consider whether you would like to be your village's main source of entertainment.) He estimates that in villages of 2000 to 6000 inhabitants, people all know each other but don't keep up with each other so much.

Stephan recommends that incomers to a village enrol their children in sports activities such as the local football club, or a music class. That way they will be known more quickly and accepted by the local people. It is ideal if parents can take part in local activities too. Stephan also suggested checking for language classes organised by the village municipality, or another village nearby, for mothers and their small children. This means the mothers do not have to find a babysitter if they want to learn the language. This can be helpful for the family to start getting to know other foreign families who have recently moved in. All of these tips can apply to moving into an urban neighbourhood too.

Fitting in time to work
As well as the practical value of having lunch provided near the school, it is worth considering whether you need to have childcare out of school hours. Does the town or village you would like to live in have this on offer and will there be places available? "The school days are really short here," one mother commented. "I fitted in a part-time job in the UK. I can't do that here." Her ten-year-old daughter comes home for lunch and often stays home for the afternoon too.

Political autonomy in villages

If you are considering moving to the country, you may be delighted to discover idyllic little Swiss villages with views to die for, reasonably priced houses and low cantonal and municipal taxes. However, the fact that the reasonably priced houses are not being snapped up by financially astute Swiss city dwellers might suggest that they are not always the easiest places for outsiders – Swiss or foreign – to settle in. Swiss towns and villages are municipalities with tax money and a great deal of political autonomy from both the cantonal government and the federal government in Bern.

The village authorities make both administrative and political decisions on all kinds of issues, from how to spend their money, or run the local school, to which foreign residents may become Swiss citizens. (Some communities put it up to the voters to decide on the suitability of each person.) The amount of money allocated to schooling can be relevant if you are going to send your children to the local school. For more information on how schooling works in different communities, please see my book, *Going Local – your guide to Swiss schooling.*[22]

Whether you live in a large town or move to the country, there are many things you can do to get to know your neighbours. These are discussed in the next chapter.

Chapter 10   Getting to know your neighbours

Getting started

How can you get off to a good start in the neighbourhood you move into? Many local people see it as up to you as the newcomer to make the first move and introduce yourself when you move in. We experienced a friendly neighbour ringing our bell to say hello when we first visited our new flat to measure it for curtains. However, because of the high value placed on independence, people are just as likely to respect your privacy and wait for you to signal that you want contact. It could be seen as nosey for existing neighbours to go up to the newcomer's door as they're just moving in, as if they want to get a look at their furniture.

Caroline is English and moved into a block of flats with her family. She experienced getting acquainted with the neighbours over time:

I rang the bell of the neighbours on the same floor and just introduced myself to the others when I met them on the stairway or the laundry room. I didn't have the courage to ring everyone's bell. And in a big block of flats you're not going to go running up and down the different flights of stairs. But the onus is on you to say

"I'm such a body. What's your name?" Once you've said hello, they'll always greet you. But you are a bit of an unknown quantity and people need time to suss you out. It wasn't until I had an operation on my shoulder that people stopped me and asked what had happened and what kind of operation had I had. They are very kind when you get to know them.

The one thing that still amuses me is how people always remember your name and use it: "*Gruezi, Frau Richardson*" or "*Hallo, Caroline.*" I struggle to remember names. My husband once commented that he thought they all have a card index for neighbour's names.

Caroline also comments that in general people are more reserved:

Your neighbours are friendly and will look after your house when you are away, and water your plants, and so on. But you are not in one another's houses all the time. There's no "just popping in" for a natter. Though in the summer time people are much more chatty in the garden.

The value of chatting to people one-to-one in their gardens, at the shops or on the staircase of the apartment block or while out walking your dog should not be underestimated. People sometimes stop for a brief chat and then as they get to know each other it can easily turn into an hour spent in the garden or the hallway between the apartments.

Getting together by invitation

Peach and coconut approaches can both be found in Switzerland, where some people will invite people they hardly know into their home and others wouldn't feel comfortable about it. Having a

coffee or a meal together tends to be a formal event, usually preced-
ed by an invitation. In my experience the exception to this was
when my children were at kindergarten. We dropped our children
off at each other's houses, and invited each other in for a coffee.
Swiss people who have lived abroad themselves may also have a
more laid-back approach, and some people just enjoy getting to
know others from around the world. It depends a lot on the individ-
uals you happen to meet.

In suburban areas, outgoing people may invite the neighbours
round to an open house for drinks. This often leads to further contact, especially among people who potentially have something in
common. Marlène moved with her family from France to Geneva.
She describes how her French mother invited her neighbours to
their apartment in Geneva after they moved in:

> My mother's an exception in my building. She's a real "peach per-
> son", as she speaks with everyone, doesn't have any distance with
> people and is full of energy. Not every neighbour came, and those
> who came were first a bit uncomfortable, but my mother broke the
> ice very quickly. So I don't think Swiss people are afraid to be in-
> vited, but they just need a friendly host who can relax them easily.

Neighbourhood gatherings

Another custom that is on the increase is the *Strassenfest* or street
party for people all living in the same street, or a barbecue or dinner
in the garden for neighbours, as described by Marlène:

> Once a year we meet because of the *fête des voisins*. It's a special
> day where everyone prepares something to eat and drink before

meeting together in the garden of the building. That's the only day where we can share more than a *Bonjour*. That's a good idea, if you do it of course, because this day makes it possible to get to know each other a bit better and it can create relations if we need something in the future.

In more traditional or rural communities there is more likely to be a village party or *Dorffest* for the whole village, rather than a party for just one street.

A preference for self-reliance

Traditionally in Switzerland, neighbours are very self-reliant and try not to bother others. A mother of teenagers even jokingly told me she would rather lay an egg herself than disturb others by asking for one. Neighbours will also not like to threaten a newcomer's independence by giving advice or help which has not been asked for, as if the newcomer "can't manage". The new person often has to signal that they would like advice or help. It may be a matter of getting to know your neighbour a bit first, to get a feeling for what you can ask (although asking for information should never be a problem).

Younger people are more likely to help each other out and I have heard of housing developments where people lend out tables for parties, or offer the use of their ovens and dishes. Christine, who is Swiss, points out that as people get older, and less mobile, they are also more willing to be dependent on others, preferably of their own generation. Where it is one-sided, people are careful to owe nothing (see box).

Build your wine collection
Olivia told the story of lending her corkscrew to her younger neighbour who was having a party. It was good for opening particularly wide-necked bottles. He returned it the next day with a bottle of wine as thanks. Heinz then said he once carried down the old paper for the rubbish collection for an elderly neighbour and bought something for her at the nearby shop. She rewarded him with an excellent bottle of wine. The helpers were happy to do so and did not necessarily expect to be so well rewarded. The fact that they were is more a sign of the feeling of obligation of the person asking for the favour.

In English, when people ask for help, they use expressions like, "Sorry to trouble you but . . ." or "Do you think you could possibly. . . . ?" I used to find Swiss students quite resistant to these polite expressions when I was teaching them English. They could not see any use for them. "If you're ever in trouble you will need them," I assured them. Now I am not so sure. People in Switzerland are well-organised to be self-reliant and practical help is mainly provided by the family and friends. They have a commitment to help their in-group and there is no need for persuasive language. They will also more readily call in the professionals than in countries with a strong "do-it-yourself" tradition.

As well as cultivating relationships with your neighbours, it may also help to meet foreigners or Swiss people from other cantons who are new to the area and interested in getting to know others fairly quickly. In my early days as a mother with a young baby in Switzerland, my family were far away and there were no young families in my neighbourhood. My support group, or "substitute family" consisted of other foreign mothers of various nationalities. We were all in the same boat and were committed to helping each other out, for example when we were ill and needed help with the children.

A friendly neighbour noticed that I was getting together with foreign mothers and commented, "That's not good for you. You need to meet Swiss people, not foreigners." She herself was very busy, working full-time. It had been easy for me to create an instant, informal support group with some of my foreign friends who had babies around the same time as me. I later got to know Swiss mothers and we helped each other out, for example with babysitting. However, it took longer for these relationships to develop.

Good fences

Underlying the ways in which neighbours interact is the concept of boundaries. All cultures need boundaries of some kind as people mark their territory, as illustrated in Robert Frost's poem, "Mending Wall", about two neighbours who keep remaking the wall that marks the division of their land. One is keener to build the walls and the other has a reluctance to create walls and questions those which exist. Switzerland is a landlocked country surrounded by foreign land rather than open sea. Many communities also have natural boundaries created by mountains and valleys. In the past these have protected them against enemies. People are very aware of boundaries.

Within the community the boundaries may be physical or psychological. If people live in a house, their "good fences" may be in the physical garden fence, and in an apartment block, their front door. Although the psychological walls or fences are a given, they can be removed, if people want them down. There is an awareness that once you start getting involved it may be difficult to get out of it again. Some neighbours do get to know each other well, helping and supporting each other, especially when they have young families, but you cannot *assume* that everyone wants to.

Boundaries within the home

Even when people are invited into each other's houses, different cultures view the boundaries within the home differently. What is "public" and what is "private"? If you are invited for dinner, should you "pitch in" by fetching things from the kitchen, or even the fridge? Probably not. I remember being very surprised when a group of Tamil women visited my home in Switzerland. After a cup of tea they all marched into the kitchen with their cups and each one washed her own. It was a gesture of thoughtfulness to save me the work. As a guest in Switzerland, you are usually not expected to go into the kitchen, or in an open-plan setting, to leave the table and head for the cooking area. At a buffet, if you ask guests to help themselves to a second helping of food from the kitchen, you may find no one moves and you have to bring it to them instead. They are respecting boundaries.

Another room which can be part of your public or private sphere is the bedroom. In Scotland, if people have a lot of visitors, they may put all the coats on the bed, and then the visitors go and fish their coats out of the pile when they are going home. In Switzerland I did this too in the early days, and a Swiss visitor to our apartment said it was all looking great, and all that was missing was a coat stand in the hall. Maybe he didn't like fetching his jacket from the bedroom.

Chapter 11   Managing conflict in the neighbourhood

Power drills and bicycles

Just as neighbours vary in the amount of contact they want with newcomers, they vary in their sensitivity to the use of shared space, be it physical or psychological. Noise seems the most common area of potential conflict, but another typical issue related to shared space is whether things are allowed to stand or lie around in front of people's house entrances. Richard is from the USA and comments that you cannot generalise about this in Switzerland. Everywhere is different. He now lives with his family in an apartment in the centre of a small Swiss city. It is multicultural living, as his neighbours come from all over the world. "The gardens are very loud on Sundays, with people even using their power drills," he said. "No one complains." He compares this with a street he used to live in where people were very strict about noise – once the police were involved in a dispute involving evening lawn mowing.

We experienced an issue with shared space when we lived in a house with a large shared garden and shared bicycle cellar. It was very full, so some of the families didn't try to squeeze their bikes into it in the evenings, as the rules specified. Instead they lined them up neatly next to the path, ready for a quick getaway in the morning. Emil, one of our few Swiss neighbours, was in his 90s and didn't really like this. He once asked me once if there was no room in the bike cellar for the bikes, looking hard at my bike outside our front door as he said it. I confirmed that there wasn't. However, what bothered him the most was the fact that some children left their bikes lying on the path overnight, because he might trip over them in the dark.

We occasionally had a barbecue outside together on a Friday evening, to which Emil was invited too. He enjoyed this very much and started having a birthday party every year, to which he invited around 20 to 30 of us. One year, he decided to tackle the bike issue. He made a speech in German and asked me to translate it into English. He read out some government statistics about the high rate of accidents leading to fractures in the over-90s like himself and the dangers of object lying on the path in the dark. He asked the parents to make sure the children put their bikes away in the evening.

One neighbour from abroad didn't feel comfortable about being told off. Her children tended to leave their bikes on the path and she commented to me afterwards that it was a bit odd to invite people to your party and then tell them off for their misdemeanours. I could see her point and knew I would have felt the same in my early days here. However, after over 20 years, I saw it more as an example of the classic Swiss comment, "It's not personal." Emil was not trying to start a fight with his request. He wanted to be on good terms with everyone, and didn't want to report the problem to the letting agent. At the same time he needed to know he could walk through the garden safely. From my perspective, keeping bikes off the path was a small price to pay for the relative freedom the children, and we, their parents, enjoyed.

Siesta time

"In Switzerland there seems to be a right time to be quiet or make a noise," a British mother commented to me. It took me a moment to realise she was talking about the rule that people should be quiet at lunch time. Switzerland doesn't come across as a typical siesta country, and it is hard to imagine the whole nation going to sleep in the middle of the day. However, there is usually a local by-law or house rule that you should not make a noise between 12 and 1 pm, (or after 10 pm, or on a Sunday), e.g. cutting your grass, drilling holes or playing the piano. In English-speaking countries there is less of a clear expectation about noise levels at different times of day.

Music practice

If you have a young family, it can also be worth looking for a child-friendly place to live where there are other young families making plenty of noise. Mike is from the USA and grew up in the suburbs there:

> We lived in single family houses over the landscape. Each had their garden, no fences, but lots of space. Houses are closer together here in Switzerland. We now live in an apartment block and find

the closeness and the lack of space a bit hard to handle sometimes. We are the only family – we also make the most noise and dirt.

In Mike's block of flats, the other owners are elderly and quite sensitive to noise, as he describes:

When our son started music lessons we suddenly became the minority. We discovered that not all musical instruments are welcome. Our son got a drum set. We talked to our neighbours and asked if we could have a time of day that it would be all right for them if he played in the cellar. That option was vetoed. Thankfully we found space to rent in a room in an old building 100 meters away. There was a cultural understanding that was surprising to us: of course you do not play that instrument in the building.

It is typical that young drummers have to find a place to drum away from the place they live. People get used to knowing detailed rules like this and following them.

Checking things out with others

When you are familiarising yourself with the house rules and local community by-laws, be aware that you *may* not have to obey everything to the letter. The extent to which rules are enforced depends on your neighbours and whether there is a strict caretaker or owner living in the building. Ursula is Swiss and suggests you check things out with a Swiss neighbour you get on well with. She lived in the USA for many years and believes that there is no point in "walking on eggs" in a new environment – not knowing what people might have problems with and guessing at what you might be able to get away with. She suggests that it is best to talk to people in the same house to find out whether it would bother them if you played the piano between 12 and 2. It might not be a problem at all for some people.

The problem for neighbours, especially older ones, may be your unpredictability as an exotic newcomer. Ursula suggests you reduce their uncertainty by giving them a chance to get to know you, chatting in the hallway, or over a cup of tea and most of them will be friendly in return. You can also reduce their uncertainty by telling them your plans. You may have read a rule telling you to be quiet after 10 pm but it will probably still be okay to have a party in your apartment on a Saturday night. Some Swiss people let their neighbours know they are going to have a party that will go on late, and tell them when it will finish. Then if the neighbours are lying awake at midnight, at least they know it will be coming to an end at a specified time and do not have to fear it could go on all night.

Older people in particular worry about standards dropping and their living quality deteriorating, so showing you are aware of the issues will reassure them. This does not mean you have to do everything they want. You have rights too. If you think people are inventing new rules, you could say "I missed that one" and check it with other local people.

Laundry room stories
Switzerland is renowned for its laundry room stories and we have all heard some good ones. I once met an Austrian woman who told me she was washing her clothes in the communal laundry room

on the allocated day (she had Mondays) but was hanging it up to dry in her rented flat. A notice suddenly appeared in the communal laundry room, saying that washing had to be hung up in the laundry room. So she hung up most of her washing in the laundry room, but still hung up her underwear in the privacy of her flat. Then a new notice appeared in the laundry room, saying "ALL washing has to be hung up in the laundry room." "Perhaps they noticed that I'm not hanging up my underwear," she said. "Shall I write and tell them I don't wear any?"

House rules and the law

Local people might complain to you about things that you are actually allowed to do. For example, Swiss law permits you to hang up your washing to dry on a stand on your balcony, but not on a rope strung across the balcony. Someone might tell you that the house rules forbid you to hang it on a stand. The house rules are wrong in this point as this is not supported by Swiss law. You are therefore allowed to keep hanging your washing on the stand. The Swiss *Beobachter* magazine and website (in German) give detailed information on this type of issue.[23]

Some issues don't go away, and many Swiss people have a personal legal protection policy for all sorts of legal disputes. This is a type of insurance policy that allows you to speak on the phone free of charge to a lawyer about the law and your rights. Some of them advise policy holders on neighbourhood cases, as well as employment law and social insurance law. This service is also available in English. I recently counted 18 different companies offering personal legal protection insurance in Switzerland.[24] It costs around 140–300 Swiss francs per year.

For some matters, like clearing away snow from pavements, the rules of the apartment block will stipulate whether the tenants have to do it. If a house is rented, it is the tenant's responsibility. In some cases, the property managers will decide when it is time to get the shovel out and clear the snow for the tenants, and this will be included in the price of services. If someone slips and falls, the party who should have cleared the snow away can be liable for any injury incurred.

Being corrected

Many local people are surprised to hear that foreigners have been told off for disobeying rules. They don't notice the rules themselves because obeying them is second nature. Out of concern for the environment, they do not leave their car engine running while they run back into the house to get something. To avoid noise pollution, they do not mow their lawn after 7 pm on a Saturday evening (or whatever the local by-law says), and not at all on a Sunday. If you are foreign and have lived here for a long time you will probably not very often be corrected for rule infringement either. It is typical of foreigners who have been here for years to believe Switzerland has changed a lot because no one corrects *them* the way they used to.

In the end, foreigners who have lived in Switzerland for a while may become more used to the rules than Swiss people who have lived abroad for a long time. Melanie recently came back to

Switzerland from her home in India, and stayed in her parents' house while they were on holiday. She was leaving very early to catch a flight home on the day the rubbish bags were collected from the street, so she put her bag out the day before. Someone rang the bell that same evening to complain to her about it. "Next time I will ask my neighbours to put the bag out for me on the correct day," she said. "I was no longer aware of how deep this goes."

Mike and his wife have now experienced being the people with a complaint, due to living so close together. He finds it important to address it directly:

> Last summer a lady moved in from abroad and became quite loud in her apartment. We spoke to her with a specific request. "We'd like you to turn down your TV while we're having dinner outside." We had to talk it through. She was quite shocked. We make noise too, and have to turn it down. We realise that people have different personalities and circumstances. The approach we take is that we have to initiate dialogue. We see the situation. How can we find a solution?

Mike is well aware that some neighbours do not address issues directly with the person concerned, but instead talk to other neighbours, who are not directly involved. Other people have reported finding an anonymous note on their car windscreen telling them their car is parked improperly. This "sneaky" approach is often taken, but is seen as a bit cowardly. It is considered more admirable in Switzerland to have "civic courage" and speak to the person directly. I heard of one case of someone sending a WhatsApp messages with a picture of a car parked in the wrong place to show their new neighbours what they were doing wrong. This is certainly a more direct approach, but I think I would prefer the person to ring my bell and talk to me face to face about what's bothering them.

It's not personal

If people do address problems face to face, part of the shock can be the way it is done. Paolo is Italian-speaking Swiss, but grew up in London. He teaches English in Ticino, and says the following:

> I do not teach my Italian-speaking Swiss students the complex sentence structures you find in some English course books, like "Do you think you could possibly . . ." or "I hope you don't mind me saying so, but . . . ." People in Ticino are not particularly loquacious and do not have much use for speaking indirectly. If someone opens the window on the train and there is a draught, the Ticinese who does not like the draught will either be shy and say nothing or tell them quite directly to close it again.

There are clear parallels here with German-speaking Swiss communication preferences. They also tend not to have much use for speaking indirectly, or manipulating the language in a complex way to ask for something. If they have a right to ask, then they can say it straight. Pointing out that people are doing something wrong should not be a personal matter. Marcel is Swiss and has lived in Canada. He compares the way people tell each other about the law:

> Below my office in Basel there is a one-way street. You often hear people yelling at drivers who are driving up it the wrong way. In

> Canada if someone wanted to tell me off for this, they would approach me with an apologetic look on their face and say politely, "Excuse me, this is actually a one-way street."

Canadians often add a personal touch to their message to soften it and save the face of the person being corrected. Thinking about the personal aspect of the interaction comes quite naturally in a peach culture, where people also relate to strangers and have little chats with them. For German-speaking Swiss, reminding someone of the rules is not meant to be personalised communication. They know they are imposing (on the other's freedom), but minimise the imposition by avoiding using any expressions which might suggest they are trying to relate to the other person, as that would detract from the matter at hand. Clear, efficient communication should have higher priority. The key issue is who is right, rather than how it is communicated. Please see also Chapter 16 on being matter-of-fact in the workplace.

Responding to criticism

Finding a way to deal with complaints or criticism is a useful skill to learn. If you are the newbie to the neighbourhood your situation could be compared with opening a new business. Early feedback is helpful and although it is unpleasant, you would like to hear from unsatisfied "customers". They might just be the tip of the iceberg. If they are in the right, it is better to be proactive and get things sorted out early.

Pat came to Switzerland from Wales and was confronted with

things every day that made her indignant. "When you walk the dog, you are told to make sure it doesn't piddle on someone's patch of grass near the street," she told me. "It made me furious. But over time it starts to be clear that it is all incredibly sensible. I have learned that I can physically dial down my indignation index. I feel a lot more peaceful."

I once went out for a walk with Pat and her dog when I saw this in practice. A woman pointed out to her that dogs were not allowed in the section of the park we were walking in. "Thank you very much," replied Pat. We then walked to the other section of the park where dogs were allowed. The woman was reminding her of a written rule. She treated the input as useful information and acted on it.

If it is more complicated than a simple rule, the ideal Swiss way to deal with it is to sit together and talk about it, perhaps with a local person as a third party to help clarify the issues. In German this kind of chat is known as a *klärendes Gespräch* and in French *une discussion ouverte*. Megan told me that she and Martin, her Swiss husband, got together for a discussion with their neighbours in the apartment below. The neighbours had complained about the noise of Megan and Martin's children running around in the apartment above their heads. It was an old building and there was little noise proofing between the floors. They came to an agreement that Megan and Martin would stop their children from running around late in the evening, as this was when it disturbed the neighbours the most.

Part four: Workplace values

Chapter 12 Swiss mountain climbing

Discussing project management

"There is too much change going on in our projects," commented a German IT specialist in a Swiss company where I was leading a training workshop. His concern was that project plans were being changed along the way by his new Anglo-American management and the project then went off in a different direction. He backed up his comment with the following argument: "Project work is like building a house. You work to a plan, you lay the foundation and then you build the cellar. You slowly work up to the roof. You can't change the plans as you go along."

When the German IT specialist suggested that a project was like building a house, my immediate reaction was to suggest a different metaphor. "For me, project work could be like going on a journey," I said. "For example, you arrive at the south of an island and work your way towards a destination in the north. The goal is clear, but how you get there is not fixed. You might walk along the beach for a while, and then if the tide comes in, climb up a cliff path and walk along the cliffs." I turned to the other participants. "How do others see it?" An American HR manager in the workshop said, "I think I can relate more to the journey idea. But the goal might change too and you change the destination."

It became clear that we all had different expectations regarding "how projects should work" and that our metaphors to express these were different. In introducing his metaphor, the German IT specialist gave his co-workers a way to express their previously unspoken and somewhat conflicting assumptions. The strong foundations and unalterable design plans related to the house building metaphor were shared and contrasted with the island journey involving the ebb and flow of the tides, finding alternative routes and mention of weather conditions and "taking down tents" during the journey.

Activity and output
The two metaphors reflected a conflict of expectations regarding both the process and the final output of a project among that particular group of people. A key issue was whether a plan can be changed once it is made. If you are "building a house", major changes should not happen. The bathroom and the living room cannot easily be switched. If you are "on a journey", you can easily take a different route, and possibly change the final destination, or goal. Alessandro from Ticino identified with these two metaphors to explain differences at his Swiss workplace. "American project management method values activity: "We're doing something. The goal could change," he said. "The Swiss value deliverables, or output, like a house you've built."

The steep Swiss mountain

I started using the idea of metaphors in my workshops as a way to start a conversation about attitudes to projects. Over the years, the most common image chosen by German-speaking Swiss groups was that of climbing a mountain. I take a closer look at this image in the rest of this chapter and discuss the role it plays in competitiveness and group thinking.

Swiss mountain pictures tend to show a process approach to project work. They usually show a clear path up a steep mountain, with a Swiss flag at the top, and the mountaineers walking in a row behind each other. Teamwork is visualised as hard work, as the mountain is steep and it is an uphill struggle. Daniel worked for many years for a German-speaking Swiss company with around 800 employees. He identifies with the metaphor of climbing a mountain in a team to reach a goal:

> It is quite far away, and requires a lot of effort. You can have the feeling you're not making progress. You wonder: "Why am I doing this to myself?" When you arrive and look back at the valley, you see that the view is wonderful and you feel happy. "Where is the next mountain?" you ask yourself. I even wrote that in to a presentation for the CEO.

While I was working on this chapter I was correcting emails written by my bachelors' students. They had to invite guests to a launch party for an imaginary new product. Many of them spelt out the hard work in their invitation: "After two years of hard work, we are now ready to launch our new Gorgeous Curls shampoo." This runs counter to my experience of a "can-do" mentality I noticed when working with American clients, who do not emphasise all the work they will have to do to achieve something. In a training course in the USA, Bob, an American told me, "If you are asked to do something to a tight deadline, it's a challenge, you want to manage it. So you say you can do it. Then it becomes expected, is considered normal."

Bob and his colleagues play down the work involved and make things look easy, so that people will trust their ability to get things done. Their Swiss colleagues then assume the Americans can do it comfortably. If you are working with Swiss colleagues, it could be to your advantage to spell out clearly the amount of work you will have to do to reach a goal or a deadline. This will also allow you to set a later deadline for completion. It may sound like complaining to you, but it will sound like realistic calculations to your Swiss colleagues. (See also Chapter 16 on being matter-of-fact.)

The predetermined route

In real life, Swiss mountain climbers have a clear goal and the route will be more or less predetermined. This reminds me of the 65,000 kilometres of walking paths in Switzerland which are clearly sign-posted with yellow signs telling you where all paths lead. If you laid out all the walking paths in a line and walked them all, it would be the equivalent of walking round the earth one and a half times. In comparison, there are 71,400 kilometres of streets in Switzerland.[25] The yellow signs tell you roughly how long the walk will take and if there is a bus stop or train station at the end of it. If the sign says it will take 4 hours 50 minutes to walk from A to B, they will not expect to do it in two hours.

The right equipment

A group of people climbing a mountain will be sure to be wearing sturdy shoes and will have a well-fitting rucksack on their backs. Many parents from other countries really notice the strong emphasis of having the right equipment in Swiss schools. A sturdy school bag that sits well on the child's back and sharpened pencils in pencil cases are requirements, as are different sets of footwear for different activities. They need slippers for the classroom, and sneakers for the sports class. If they go on a day trip, they will need walking shoes and a well-fitting rucksack. Having the right equipment is a prerequisite to doing a good job wherever you are.

I noticed how "Swiss" I have become when I attended a French course in France for two weeks. At the weekend we went on a day trip to an island. We were going to do a bit of walking there and had to take a picnic with us. I realised that I hadn't brought a rucksack and immediately rushed out to buy one in a local supermarket, so as to be properly equipped for the occasion. When we got off the ferry to the island, I noticed that most of the other foreign women just had their picnics in their shoulder bags and one woman even had hers in a little plastic bag. You just don't see Swiss people going hiking, swinging their little plastic bags containing their lunch.

Competitiveness

Swiss mountain drawings do not usually show different climbing teams in a race to the top. It may appear to just be a race against time, before nightfall. Competition tends to be played down, but it can be there in the background. While I was writing this chapter, I watched a student present her bachelor's thesis on her Swiss company's marketing strategy in the face of increasing competition. The company makes products for process automation. She drew attention to the photo in her opening slide. It was a photo of four mountaineers walking along a narrow ridge near the peak of a snow-capped mountain. She said it represented her company at the top of its sector, where the air is thin. They are no competitors to be seen. They have been "left behind down in the valley", as her company offers the best products and services in the sector.

Group thinking

The mountain climbing pictures drawn by German-speaking Swiss groups always show several people, and the team leader is usually not clear from the picture. They don't represent their differences in their mountain drawings. They are all mountain climbers. In Chapter 13 interviewees describe how decisions sometimes get made by consultation in their companies. In many cases, it is not the leader who decides.

I spoke about this to Richard, an American who often goes climbing in Switzerland. It makes sense to him that the mountain climbers are portrayed as a team and that the leader is not clearly marked in the drawings. He would even go as far as to say that an informal leader often emerges in a climbing trip. "If one person says, 'I feel uncomfortable. We're going back,' then we all go back, for example, if there is danger of an avalanche." The leader will not force people to keep going if they are not happy about it.

Occasionally the climbers are tied together by ropes, but more often not. This may have negative connotations for some of the people drawing the pictures (see the box *Helping your friends*). In German these roped teams are known as *Seilschaften*, and this term is used symbolically to refer to people's strong ties to others. Ropes are stronger than the net of a network, which is, as I realised recently, full of holes. The ropes are symbolic of the climbers supporting each other.

Helping your friends
The term *Seilschaften*, or roped teams, can be used to refer to people getting help from friends to get a "leg up" somewhere, for example, if they lose their job and need to find a new one. (And a leg up is literally what you need, if you are starting to slip down the mountain.) In Switzerland, the rope ties can refer to anyone who knows and trusts the character and competence of a friend or colleague. They may be able to tip off the job seeker about an opening in their company, and also recommend the job seeker to the recruiters. This is hard for those who do not have these contacts, and they may use the *Seilschaften* term as a criticism of those who do.

The ropes concept can be used positively. Hans explains that someone may have more experience and informally share their knowledge and skills with others. If they see that someone is going about something in the wrong way, they can warn them and help them, by pulling them back when they slip. Daniel told me about a team-building event he organised to help a new team in his company to gel with each other:

> I chose the symbolism of a *Seilschaft* going up a mountain together. I gave each team member a carabiner hook which you use to attach your harness to the rope joining you to the other climbers. The rope symbolises the fact that you have to move forward together if you want to get somewhere. It is impossible to climb the mountain alone. Everyone has to do their bit. You need to be willing to take others with you.
>
> As the leader you can be an enabler, but you do not pull the rope

along. People have to be motivated to walk. It has to be a relationship of trust. If you don't concentrate, it is difficult. If three people are not concentrating, and one takes a step down the mountainside, he pulls everyone with him. They all need to be committed, reliable, competent, ready to work, to go the extra mile, and to support others in the team.

Chapter 13 Participative decision-making

Richard described how a leader on a Swiss climbing trip will listen to everyone's opinion in connection with decisions about safety issues (see Chapter 12). This type of participative approach to decision-making is also reported by people working in traditional Swiss companies and in some international companies headquartered in Switzerland too. There are of course many situations where decisions are made on a higher level and people are told what they have to do. This chapter explores the type of situations where employees also have a say. The examples were reported by my interviewees because their colleagues found it surprising. Chapters 14 and 15 go on to discuss related aspects, addressing types of leadership and people taking charge of their own work.

Let's vote

Melanie Martinelli used to work in India for a software company. She once travelled with her Indian boss to German-speaking Switzerland to discuss changes to specifications in software they were designing for a Swiss client. The biggest surprise for her boss was how patient he had to be with the Swiss. She explains how the decision-making process was slow and confusing to him:

> Our client was an IT provider. They had run out of money so they wanted to take some of the functionalities out of the software we were designing for them, to reduce the costs. They analysed each aspect and everyone had a different view. In the last ten minutes the Swiss boss said, "Now we have enough information. Let's vote on it." My Indian boss didn't understand that. What was the point of discussing and then voting? They could just do an online survey and send out everyone's standpoint and then vote. Why should he fly in from India to watch them vote?
>
> My boss thought the person who's paid more should assume responsibility. For him, bosses seem to be very weak in Switzerland. On the way back to India he wondered if the company had even made the wrong decision. Do low level people understand the business strategy? For him, the boss was dumping responsibility for the decision on people who are paid less and have less knowledge.

Melanie sees the degree to which bosses give responsibility to lower level people as a cultural challenge for technical specialists coming from India to work in Switzerland:

> Techies from India lose respect for Swiss bosses. They see them as lazy and not knowledgeable when they delegate the decision-making process. In India, experienced technically-skilled people are promoted. In Switzerland it is not necessary for bosses to have more knowledge. They need managerial skills and can be young.

A consensus-finding process

Melanie and her boss experienced a Swiss team voting, but group decisions may also be made without taking a vote. Emilia is American and experienced this when she started a new job with a start-up company in German-speaking Switzerland. She would have preferred more guidance to be provided by her Swiss manager:

> Our manager doesn't sound the bell as to our vision, or raise the flag to set a clear direction for the group. It is more of a consensus-finding process. He just throws out his ideas. We were in a process where we were going to have to replace equipment used by our clients and we needed to inform them. Our manager wanted to create a standard letter, or a brochure, and send it out. He said, "One size fits all." Others said, "It needs to be customised." They wanted to discuss it more. "Customise in what way?" someone asked. And someone else said, "We need to do it with the minimum overhead." I watched from the outside. In the end they decided to do a brochure and customise it. This was actually not what the boss wanted. It didn't make sense to me.

Consult before your pitch

In both of the cases above, the decision-making process took place at the meeting itself. If roles are clearly defined, important consultations with key players may take place in advance of meetings, as this is more efficient. This approach is illustrated by Daniel, who is on the management board of his medium-sized Swiss company:

Let's say our communication team is preparing an advertising campaign for a new product and want to make our pitch to the management board meeting to get the budget. First I have to check with the head of sales whether it fits with their processes. Then I have a talk with the Chief Digital Officer and he will give me some input regarding the platform. So when I go to the management board meeting I can say explicitly that I have already discussed it with these people, who are present at the meeting. It then goes through smoothly. If I can't say that I've checked our ideas with others, the CEO will refuse to let me present it. He will reject it out of hand.

Chantal has experienced this way of working in her traditional Swiss company as a humble approach:

If you lead a project in Switzerland, you are asked to involve several people. In France I do it on my own, with my own thoughts, to go in a specific direction. Here I have to take the humble position. "This is my approach. What do you guys think?" We build the project and the solution together. In one way, it's a really good working atmosphere. The decision is not just based on one opinion. Everyone feels involved.

Back stage consultations

Surprisingly, a participative approach is also common in international companies in Switzerland, even if everyone is speaking English and there are no local Swiss people around. It may take place "back stage", which can make it hard for newcomers to be aware of it. The following examples are from Matej and Lorna, who each work for a different international healthcare company in

Switzerland. Matej is Slovenian and works in HR. He compares the approach to decision-making in his company in Switzerland and in Slovenia:

> In Slovenia, if we had a meeting and had to prepare a presentation or proposal, we'd enter the room, present it, answer questions, debate it, and the decision would be taken in the meeting.
>
> Some people would agree or disagree, and either the leader or the majority would decide the way forward and everyone would go with that.
>
> What surprised me eight years ago when I came to Switzerland was that here you reach agreement with everyone in advance before giving your presentation. It's called an "alignment and consensus approach". It's not recommended that you surprise people with something they're not aware of. If they are taken by surprise in a meeting, they will say "no".
>
> So let's say I want to run a competency assessment across business units. I discuss it with the boss or business partner in advance to find out their concerns and align and convince them that this is the way forward. If they are convinced, they will be advocates of it, or at least say "I can live with that." In the meeting, the only questions are for clarification. You need the ability to sell your story and be part of the story yourself in the way you engage with others, without being forceful.

Matej is of course using the word "surprise" negatively, as it is often used in German-speaking Switzerland. People tend not to like surprises at work. They like to have time to think things over and get used to them. Lorna is British and refers to the process of getting alignment in her company as "pre-vetting":

The pre-vetting of ideas is important. If you have a project and need a committee to sign off on the budget or the strategic direction, you will present it at a meeting to get their official buy-in. But the meeting is just a formality. They just say, "Yes, yes, here's your budget". What you actually do is have a coffee and a chat with the committee members individually beforehand and show them your slides on your laptop. You ask them if they have any input, and embed their ideas in your presentation. Some people come in from other companies and just go straight into the meeting with a great presentation. They have not spoken to anyone about it and get taken apart.

The way Matej and Lorna describe the process makes it sound a bit like a wedding ceremony. The main decision was made beforehand and everyone expects the bride and groom to just say, "I do." They are not expected to start fleshing out the details of their agreement during the ceremony.

You may find yourself in a similar situation, presenting to a committee or a group of business unit heads. It is important to find out whether there is anyone you should be speaking to about your proposal before you present it. It could even be that you are told to speak to someone who doesn't seem very important and you underestimate that person's advice as an informal opinion leader who is very influential and respected by the group.

Swiss processes abroad

Swiss participative approaches are also followed by Swiss companies in other countries. Natascha works in communication for an international company at its Swiss head office, and told me about Rani, a new colleague who had started work in a communication role at their UK site. Rani was a bit confused by the complexity of the review processes the company follows when an important communication goes out to the company's employees. There are usually many people who have something to say about the content and it takes time to reach agreement on this. Natascha offered to show Rani their review process documents, which show how to go about it. It may take some figuring out, but at least her company has something in writing for newcomers to read up on.

The sanding down process

Although people may try to reach consensus in advance of – or in – their meeting, it is not always possible. Then there is either a vote or the boss decides. Matej comments, "If consensus is not reached, everyone turns to the boss and he or she says 'there's the direction we'll go in'. Someone has to call it." For some topics in Daniel's more traditional Swiss company it is really important that everyone agrees. "The content is sanded down (in German: *geschliffen*) to make it acceptable to everyone," he explained.

Swiss political culture
This Swiss approach to decision-making reflects aspects of Swiss politics. Sylvie Chevrier's study of French multinational corporations suggests that employees in French-speaking Switzerland actively seek consensus at a grassroots level.[26] She argues that

Swiss people share a common political culture based on government through consensus and solving conflicts by resorting to arbitration and pragmatism. She states that management practices are embedded in national political cultures.

Switzerland has no prime minister or head of state. The Swiss Federal Council is the highest executive authority in the country. It is made up of seven members from four different political parties, with one acting as president for one year only. They follow an unwritten principle of collegiality and talk through the views of all four represented parties. Once they have made a decision, all members of the Council defend the decision to the press and the public. A distinction is made between consensus – where everyone has agreed – and the collegial principle, where some do not agree with the result, but present it to the public as one voice. Normally the public do not hear who voted for or against.

In other countries, people might use the word "consensus" if there is broad agreement but it is not unanimous. In Switzerland, consensus in the sense of unanimity can be achieved by the sanding down process described by Daniel.

Giving suppliers a say

Chantal also consults with external service providers who are affected by internal change in her Swiss company:

Right now we are organising several changes in the way we work and the technology we use. We will involve internal colleagues and even external partners. In France we would tell the external service provider, "Now you have to work this way." In Switzerland we say, "Now we'd like to have your opinion so we can decide together." We should involve them because they will have to learn to use it. It's a procedure I'm used to now. It has become natural for me and I really love it. But it does require energy and time.

Chantal admits that in the end the external service provider will have to do what the company decides. "But they can express their views and try to influence the way we are going to work together."

Forming allegiances

Getting people on side may involve a fair bit of networking. Melanie describes how people form allegiances and influence others in decision-making in Switzerland and India:

> In Switzerland you lobby for your cause and try to convince people. You have a pros and cons discussion over lunch. People want to have equal opportunities to influence each other and build allies. It is important who you have coalitions with when a decision needs to be taken. In India, people support others they are close to – family and friends. They say, "I'll go with your idea because I like you more."

If you are hired to implement a new strategy in one division of a company, for example, HR or IT, you may be making changes in a division that provides a service to other divisions. You may need to actively engage key people in the other divisions to get them on side. This may also be the case if your brief comes directly from the CEO. A Swiss CEO will not necessarily instruct everyone across the board to do what you tell them. It may be up to you to ask their opinion as suggested by Matej and Lorna, and win them for the cause by yourself. This may involve adjusting your new strategy to their needs.

Creative input in Romandie

Differences are reported between French and French-Swiss leadership styles. Charles is French and has worked for several years in product development for a company in Romandie. His division was quite small when he joined it and his French-speaking Swiss colleagues were used to having a say in decision-making. Soon after he arrived, they got a new French boss who made very clear unilateral decisions to cancel projects that he considered to have no future. Charles's Swiss colleagues wanted the opportunity to be creative and innovative, and found it difficult that they were no longer being invited to make a contribution to the problem-solving:

> It was fine for me that the new boss made the decisions, but my Swiss colleagues had a lot of trouble accepting it. They wanted to discuss it with him. "Maybe we should consider this option or that one, or maybe we should have a working session to analyse different options." The French boss was not pleased. He said, "That's it. Decided. Move on". It didn't go well for him at first. It's typical of Swiss culture to want to discuss everything and compromise.

Charles reported that, with time, the style of the new French boss became the approach taken across the company division:

> Now the division has evolved. We are much bigger and more international and we have much more of a top-down approach. We need this as we have a lot of initiatives going on and a lot of

strategies to be executed. We need to deliver and can't have extensive discussions from below. About 60 to 70% of employees agree with this. About 30 to 40% don't. They just give up and don't ask so many questions.

Directive German leadership

A study was conducted with 252 German and Swiss participants in Swiss companies and included the topic of leadership styles.[27] Two main leadership styles were reported: a participative Swiss leadership style and a directive German leadership style. The "Swiss" style involved trying to integrate all needs and interests of employees while the "German" style involved giving very clear instructions, exerting pressure and setting tight deadlines. In practice, the Swiss style was reported to be much more common, also among Germans in Switzerland. Most participants, whether German or Swiss, preferred the Swiss leadership style and were critical of the German style. The conflicts this caused were related specifically to different hierarchical levels. When asked about their relationships to colleagues on the same level, the survey participants reported that there were few conflicts.

The Swiss-Indian combo sandwich

It can be quite tricky to get the balance in leadership if you have a participative style and your employees are used to a more directive style, or vice versa. Melanie explains the approach she takes:

In the early years running my company in India, I didn't lead my team the way they wanted. They were frustrated and would ask me "Why don't you tell me how to do it?" It took me years to learn it, but now I ask them open questions, "How could you do it? What are your ideas?" Then I conclude "I've considered it all and this is the way we'll go." They like contributing. They appreciate the mix, the Swiss-Indian combo sandwich. It shows you care about them and are trying to help them develop.

This chapter has considered how employees and even suppliers may be encouraged to participate in decision-making. This requires a particular type of leadership style which is reported to be more common in German-speaking Switzerland than in Romandie or Ticino. This will be discussed in the following chapter.

Chapter 14   Transactional and transformational leadership

Implementing swift change

Mateo was a change manager who was hired by a fast-growing Swiss company to swiftly introduce big changes. It was important to Mateo to identify who was on side, with him and willing to go the extra mile for him. However, he was having difficulty getting his top team together. He had previously worked in Latin America, and there, if a senior executive wished to meet his top team, they would all clear their calendars immediately to make it possible:

> When I'm arranging meetings with the Swiss, the guys are already booked, they can't make the meeting. People have their calendars laid out for the year. There is no reason to change it. I don't understand that line. It took a week just to get the date for the team meeting. How much can I push?

Were Mateo's Swiss team genuinely worried about cancelling their other appointments and letting people down or were they resisting change? It might have been a bit of both. Metaphorically speaking, he was being asked to take "mountain climbers" on a fast-paced journey into the unknown.

Mateo started to take the approach of arguing for business needs as the driver for a new way of working. "The system requires XYZ" is a more convincing argument in German-speaking Switzerland than "I want XYZ." In other words, "You don't have to do it because I want you to (although I do), but because it's the best way to do the job."

Incomers are often hired to work for Swiss companies when major changes are to be implemented swiftly and forcefully from the top. Local change managers may be reluctant to take on the role. Announcing to local people that there are exciting times ahead and that you are planning some big changes is not seen as the quickest way to get them on side. They are more used to the salami tactic. This is where you keep cutting off a little slice of salami over a period of time and let people slowly get used to the shrinking salami, rather than making the whole salami disappear at once. It is unpleasant and people moan about it, but they have time to adjust. The salami tactic is being used these days with Swiss retirement pensions, which are expected to slowly decrease in value over the coming years.

"Actionism"

"Actionism" is a word typically used to criticise decisions made quickly, followed by rapid change. KPMG magazine reported on the issue of the strong Swiss franc being a challenge for Swiss businesses exporting their goods. It quoted Hans-Ulrich Bigler, Director of the Swiss Federation of SMEs (Small and Medium Enterprises) talking about action to be taken.[28] He advised against *"hektische Aktionismus"* in German (hectic activism) and *"actionisme febrile"* (feverish activism) in French. His comment is translated into English as "We need to increase our focus on tried and tested policies instead of *pointless unfocused action*." The German and French terms could make Swiss locals think of hasty measures without a thorough analysis of their probable efficacy.

Reflect, analyse, prepare

Elizabeth is an English project leader in a Swiss healthcare company. She has worked there for many years, and considers herself to have a "Swiss approach". Her company was recently taken over by an American company and she describes her perspective of the change in management style she has recently experienced. "With the new management there is a quickness at a higher level. They're going in this direction, then suddenly, they're off in another direction." She gives an example of resistance from her team to change in the speed of getting a drug to market:

The new management regard us as change-blockers. For example, they decided to be more aggressive about approval dates, the time it takes to get a new drug approved by the authorities. We estimate that it will take longer because we have a buffer built in and we tell them this. In my company you reflect, analyse, prepare. The work has gone in up front before you set off on the journey, or design the house. You have resources, material, prediction of time lines. They say we're overanalysing the problem and are too slow. They pride themselves on their speed of executing. In their company culture it is more important to act quickly, and more acceptable to get it wrong.

Swiss leadership study

It could be said that Mateo and Elizabeth's management were taking a *transformational* approach to leadership, which is defined as "mobilizing and energizing followers, creating an agenda for action and focusing on shared goals".[29] A study in the Swiss banking sector concluded that *transactional* leadership is more effective in German-speaking Switzerland than in other parts of the country, and is seen to be based on the task and employees' performance.[30] People work fairly independently, rules and standards are frequently observed, and a leader only intervenes if standards are not met. You do not exercise power for its own sake. A good German-speaking Swiss boss should not be charismatic, but needs to be prepared to quietly and calmly defend their ideas in the face of criticism or opposition.

According to the banking sector study, transformational or charismatic leadership is more effective in Italian and French-speaking Switzerland. Employees there are more likely to accept that power is exerted over them than in German-speaking Switzerland. This includes leaders motivating and inspiring others in a way that their followers wish to emulate them. The leader's physical presence is expected and valued. The leader must be also able to address and manage ego-related emotions such as frustration.

The study reports that there is a strong emphasis on encouraging employees to be creative and innovative in French-speaking

Switzerland. This was touched on in Charles' example of his colleagues who wanted to be help their boss find solutions to problems. In Italian-speaking Switzerland, leadership is seen to be based on *"autorevolezza"*, or charisma, and respect and trust are very important. Relationships between superiors and subordinates are close and personal.

> **French respect for superiors**
> In a study of a French company, a French-speaking Swiss employee commented that French employees had more respect for their superiors than Swiss employees did. Swiss managers were more likely to accept advice from a subordinate than French managers were.[31] Swiss managers did not like to have impressive-sounding job titles for the sake of status, but liked their job title to reflect their actual tasks.
>
> The one thing that was emphasised by all Swiss in the study was that working practices are derived from the participative culture of Switzerland's direct democracy. It was clear from the study that the company culture at the Geneva office was the closest to the company culture of the French headquarters, as many French nationals worked in Geneva.

Being the boss in Ticino

I talked about the banking study with Alessandro from Ticino. He has worked for many years for a company based in Zurich, with subsidiaries in Ticino and Geneva. He agrees that transformational management fits for both places:

In Ticino and Geneva, the boss is really the boss, a higher being. You have to stand up in front of the people and inspire them. This is not expected in German-speaking Switzerland. There is a more horizontal participative leadership style.

You have to tell people from Ticino or Milan that your idea is not meant as an instruction. If I just want to explore some ideas with them, I have to say, "I am just brainstorming." Otherwise the person takes it seriously and starts carrying it out immediately. You have to coach people so that they feel authorised to say what they think, or to correct you. As a boss, it's very easy to do things wrong if they don't correct you.

Lobbying for projects

Transformational leadership involves "mobilising and energising followers". Transactional leadership, in contrast, is more likely to involve employees mobilising and energising themselves. This involves being self-directed. Once someone has said they will do something, it is like a verbal contract, and sticking to it is a sign of a good character. This can be very different elsewhere. I spoke to a German scientist in the USA who had been sent there for a year by her Swiss company. She told me that she felt like a dog on a lead at the American site. In Switzerland, if she committed to delivering data to a project by a certain date, she knew she would do it. However, the American project leader would contact her before the deadline and ask how things were going and if she needed any help with anything. From her perspective, he didn't trust her to get the job done, although she had said she would.

A project leader I spoke to in the USA described this approach as "lobbying" for his projects. From his perspective, people are under a lot of pressure juggling tasks for different people and might have trouble meeting their deadline for some of them. It is his job as the leader to keep people informed, get regular updates, find out about any problems, and help them deliver on time:

> It helps if everyone understands the timetable for a process. Sometimes you give a little bit of detail behind the scenes as to why you're asking for information at a certain time. It's not just you're picking this out of the air; there's a timetable there that you're maintaining that they don't see. So just be transparent about the processes.
>
> The more informal contact that you make, the better informed you are, and the better the team members feel. When you check things out informally, that means that you call into someone's office, or have a coffee or lunch, or just meet at the water cooler. If I'm in the same building I'll make sure I pop in if their office door is open and just sort of catch up a little bit. Cafeteria, hallway, printer, wherever you catch them. You strike up a conversation. Typically you grab five minutes of their time, and once again, usually face to face is the best. If it's team members who are at other sites, you know, that's usually a phone call, taking time zones into account.

From a Swiss perspective, "checking things out informally" could seem like nagging and, as the German scientist said, showing a lack of trust in people. Swiss leaders will leave people to get on with it. They are likely to only find out something is wrong when the deadline has passed and the results have not been delivered. Then they ask for them as a matter of urgency and people have to scramble to send them as soon as possible.

Drop-dead deadlines

This type of situation is not made easier by working virtually. I spoke to Evelyn, an American who told me about missing a deadline in Project C, a project that did not seem to be very high priority, as Evelyn and her team in the USA never heard from the project leader in Switzerland. They prioritised other projects whose leaders were in their building in the USA and who were in touch regularly, asking for progress reports. They only discovered the urgency of Project C close to the deadline, when the Swiss-based project leader suddenly got in touch and was upset to hear that they would not be able to deliver their results on time. "It turned out to have been a drop-dead deadline," said Evelyn.

I was intrigued by the term "drop-dead deadline" and Evelyn explained that it meant that her team had to do everything to meet the deadline, including working overtime, in the evenings and at weekends. After that, I started to encourage people in the company back in Switzerland to lobby more for their projects and to add "drop-dead" to their timeline vocabulary to show how serious they were about their deadlines. It is also a good idea to have regular milestones to ask about progress along the way.

The squeaky wheel

Jane, an American, heard the Project C story and commented, "Everyone knows the squeaky wheel gets the oil." She went on to explain: "If you make enough noise, you will get heard. You're more of a headache, and they'll have to deal with you. Otherwise you're at the end of the line. Out of sight, out of mind."

Reassuringly, the similarity in the two countries – Switzerland and the USA – is that if people are over-subscribed and ask for help in their tasks, they will probably get it. In the USA the need may be picked up early by someone checking how they are doing. In Switzerland people often have to take the initiative to ask for help. This is discussed further in Chapter 15 on prioritising.

Mistakes and their consequences

If you are self-directed, is there not a risk that you are over-exposing yourself and could make a mistake that could cost you your job? Angelo works out of Geneva for an Italian company based in Milan and talks about the importance of trust in this regard:

> In American companies in Switzerland they have to justify why they're firing you. They adapt a bit to Swiss ways. But the fear of being fired is there. When I had a Swiss boss I didn't fear this. He had confidence in me. "I trust my people," he said. After I had been there a week, he went on holiday, and left me to launch a project with our wholesalers. I knew that if I didn't get it right, I wouldn't be fired. I have a similar attitude to my current team in Milan. If I acquire a new client and pass them to my team, I leave them to make the decisions. They will get back to me if there is a problem, or something needs to be discussed.

Nathan works in Romandie and is very impressed with how mistakes are handled in his company:

> I was meant to send a wire transfer for 100,000 Swiss Francs to the USA. I put one zero too many on it. I had too much going on and

didn't have time to pay attention to detail. In the UK they would have fired me. My box would have immediately been put on my desk with a letter saying "Bye".

In Switzerland they take a pragmatic approach. They say, "Let's look at what went wrong, and sort it out so we don't make the same mistake again." They look at my mistake and think, "He just had too much to do. We need this guy, but we really need him to be focused on other things, not the admin stuff." So they got me an assistant who works three days a week for me. I'm in a cut-throat industry and this is the first time I have not felt afraid of being fired. When I worked in London I felt it every day.

Chapter 15 Setting priorities

Last minute action

Being self-directed means that Swiss-based employees may expect to set their own work priorities and choose exactly which tasks to do when. It can be a shock to bosses from abroad if they are seen as "jumping the queue" if they make a last minute request. Angus is Scottish and has worked for a Swiss company for many years. He has difficulty with the way his new boss from an English-speaking country allocates tasks:

My boss gives me new work, needing it done by the afternoon. That is rare in our company, that you suddenly ask for something to be done the same day. So I have to say to my team that my boss had asked me for something urgently. It comes as a surprise to people. She is new, and still learning the job. She apologises, "Sorry, Angus."

I'm flexible about it. I just think, "Okay, it has to be done." I set aside my other priorities to get it done on time. Then I encourage her next time I'm chatting with her: "If you could give me more notice . . . ." Or I explain to her: "The quality of my work may not be as good as you want. I have to go and ask people for input."

Or I tell her: "I've already promised someone else to finish their thing." If it's a bigger piece of work, I'd say I can't do it because of this or that. I'm trying to keep the balance of my reputation, my trustworthiness. It can also be a test of obedience, whether I am willing to drop everything for her.

Jumping the queue
Angus's story reminds me of a German personal assistant attending my course who told us about her new English boss asking her, "If you have time, could you type up this document before you go home?" She said, "Yes, if I have time." The next morning he came and asked for the document. "I didn't do it," she replied. "I didn't have time." She said he seemed quite surprised. An English course participant suggested that the "If you have time" bit was probably just a polite way to phrase an instruction. He was the boss and had expected it to be done. An American participant said he always expressed such requests using "I", for example, "I need this today." Then it would be clear to her that she had to do it.

Looking ahead

Alexandra is German-speaking Swiss and worked in an American company in Geneva for many years. She commented on Angus's boss expecting him to attend to her tasks first:

This may happen in an international company, where higher level management is not Swiss. It might be that Angus's boss has to take her contribution and deliver to an even higher person. Then it's understandable. In my American company in Geneva it always happened that you can't meet deadlines. So many things are outsourced. You can get stuck somewhere. It's not your fault. You just need to communicate it to your boss in advance.

In a Swiss company she's a bad boss if she asks you to do something at such short notice, no matter what impact this has on your team members. German-speaking Swiss have a strong feeling or a need for security. They look much more to the future and the past, and not so much to the present. We grow up prioritising things. We are used to looking ahead. If you do that, you automatically prioritise things without thinking too much. Others only start thinking when a problem occurs. I get frustrated and can't believe they didn't communicate earlier that a deadline now can't be met. They think, "The problem only came up now."

Realistic deadlines

Daniel recognises that prioritising is a big challenge in his Swiss company and that people can't always get it right:

> I tell my team, "You will have conflicts in setting priorities." Sometimes I recognise that it was me who caused the conflict and the work piled up. Then I say to people, "Come to me early, so that we can redistribute tasks. Don't wait until it's too late." Normally I give realistic deadlines. I don't say I want something in two days if I need it in two weeks. If I need it urgently, I explain why. Or else we have a bilateral discussion. When could they have it ready by?

Like Evelyn's team in the last chapter, employees who work on different projects may find themselves with tight deadlines for different people at the same time. They can end up in a bit of a pickle and with a lot of overtime if the requestors are not aware of others' needs. Then their line manager may need to help them work out who should be at "the front of the queue". Baris is a Swiss project assistant for various projects and explains how he manages this:

> If I have presentations to prepare for 3 different project managers and they all ask me to do things with tight deadlines close to each other, I would first ask each of them if this is the final deadline. And do they need a completed, detailed presentation by then, or just the concept? If I still can't deliver full quality to all within the time-line, I will discuss the priorities with my line manager. He will talk to them and sort it out or tell me to communicate with them all and let them know what else I'm working on and for who. If they're all higher than my line manager, he can't tell them how to sort it out. He will ask them to discuss it among themselves.

Adrenalin versus stamina in Ticino

Daniele from Ticino admits that he finds it harder to get staff from German-speaking Switzerland to do something for him at the last minute:

> They are more structured, and do not want to depart from their plan for the day. They often don't see the urgency. I expect resistance if I force something through. I need to have a good reason why. I explain why, but do not apologise. That would be an emotional approach and it needs to be communicated on a rational level.
>
> In Ticino, if I ask for something, they take more the approach, "The boss needs to have it now. There will be good reasons." You don't ask questions – whether the boss really needs it. That would be a betrayal.

Daniele experienced an interesting difference between German-speaking Swiss and Ticinese recruits in the army:

> Ticinese are world-class at getting out of difficulties. We are unbeatable in task force mode. We are sprinters, with adrenalin, not marathon runners, with stamina and consistency. That's more like the German-speaking Swiss climbing the mountain. In my company in Zurich there was no one in the offices after 6.15 pm. In Ticino they would still be there at 8 or 9 if they were needed in an emergency, no problem. They do not complain if they have to work longer.
>
> We once had a case in Ticino where we had to work late, and even a mother of a young child sat there till 1 am entering transactions in the computer. No one said, "We really don't want to." They don't have much of a sense of competition, more a togetherness. The German-Swiss are more individualist about getting work completed.

An outlet for competitiveness

When Daniele was talking about the sense of togetherness of Ticinese employees, he commented jokingly that the Ticinese have more lawyers than inhabitants. He saw this as an example of them living out their competitive side outside the company. "They have a lot of stress with each other in their neighbourhoods. They fight over their gardens and their trees, and so on." This could be said of other parts of Switzerland too.

Another outlet for Swiss competitiveness can be found in board and card games. When my brother and his family were visiting us from Scotland, we often played Phase 10, a competitive card game, in the evenings. They were quite shocked to experience the ruthlessness of my gentle Swiss husband, as he gleefully handed them cards to make them sit out the game for a round. In contrast, all the Scots were very apologetic when they had to make other people sit out. In English a card game can be referred to as a "pastime". It is not the World Cup final. In Switzerland, (especially) men playing cards or board games may openly express their satisfaction at winning and making others lose.

Helping colleagues

It is not only an urgent request from the boss that can make people change their plans. Emmanuelle, a French employee in a company in German-speaking Switzerland, told me about her role as team leader:

> If we are working on a task to a tight deadline, and someone in my team suddenly has a technical problem, we can't always rely on the IT solutions provided by the outsourced helpdesk. So I stop everything to help the person and give support in an emergency. Then I perhaps miss a meeting and I'm considered by my Swiss colleagues to be a person who doesn't respect appointments. When I am the one who is looking for help, people will tell me, "I can't do it. I have other things."

Waiting tables

Emmanuelle was very supportive of her team, helping them in an emergency. Her colleagues, on the other hand, only felt responsible for their own work. It reminds me of different approaches to waiting tables in restaurants. In a Basel restaurant you usually have "your waiter", who will serve you and bring your bill. Delia, a Basel waitress, told me "I know I have the responsibility for these tables. I can ask people to help, but in the end they are mine."

In contrast, in Italy and France, and also in Geneva, I have experienced being served by various people. They were sharing the tables. Emmanuelle is probably working in a company where she is expected to "wait her own tables", and she is really going out of her way if she also waits others' tables too. Other people will not have this frame of mind, and will not see Emmanuelle's "tables" as their responsibility.

Cancelling in advance

Savannah is Swiss and explains how she has to manage conflicting priorities in her international company:

> In my company, if it's NOT an emergency, it's a no-go to cancel a meeting at very short notice to help a colleague with a deadline. People will say, "I bet she knew about that deadline before." You have to go to the meeting, or cancel 24 hours in advance with a reason, just like cancelling a doctor's appointment. This shows you've assessed the situation in advance and give enough warning.
>
> It might also be the case that you get last minute work that IS extremely urgent and you really do have to cancel other things. Then it is better to communicate the reason very clearly. If the situation arises on Friday morning and the deadline is the evening, you can change all your appointments to "tentative" in your

calendar and put in the reason as a comment, for example, "Urgent deadline but will try to come." When you prioritise, you are saying to someone, "This other thing is more important than your issue at the moment." You need to do enough explaining to make that acceptable.

If it happens regularly that your team has technical problems, it might help to enable them to fix them by themselves or send them on a course to improve their skills. If you always do it for them, they'll still be helpless the next time it happens.

Chapter 16   Being matter-of-fact

When Angelo started working out of Geneva for a small Italian company, he experienced a different approach to feedback than he was used to. He attended meetings in Milan where the boss would shout at employees in front of 15 other people:

> "You haven't done your job!" he would yell. Everyone would sit in silence. You shout to show that you're the boss. "I went too far this time," he commented to me once. "You never get angry, do you?" "I can shout if you like," I offered, "and express my Latin side [*sortir mon côté Latin*]." But I prefer not to. I prefer to measure the effectiveness of my employees or colleagues at the end of the year and put forward all their mistakes or weaknesses which need to be improved rather than to shout at them.

Looking and sounding harmless

Angelo chose not to use emotions as a form of feedback. It can be experienced as an infringement of shared space in Switzerland and emotions tend to be played down at work. If a Swiss person says in English, "I was a little bit surprised that he didn't come to the meeting," this could actually mean that they were annoyed. The word "surprised" sounds more neutral than "annoyed", and plays down the criticism. In Swiss German, "a little bit" is expressed using the diminutive "li" (as in *es bitzeli*) as a way to sound more harmless. The many diminutives used in Swiss German make speakers sound more modest and unassuming, which is appreciated. (This reminds me of Scots using the word "wee", meaning "little", almost as a term of endearment to describe things like a wee drink, a wee cake, a wee boy or a wee girl.)

Swiss bosses are often reported to take a cautious, understated approach to giving negative feedback. A German doctor who had worked at the University Hospital in Basel told me that she had noticed a big difference in the communication style of doctors and students in Switzerland compared to Germany:

Junior doctors from Germany are used to being shouted at by the consultants (senior doctors) there, but this rarely happens in Switzerland. At our hospital, if the consultant came to speak to you and just said, "What happened?" then you knew you were in trouble. If she sat down to ask you what had happened, you know you were in *serious* trouble.

There was also a difference in the way students expressed themselves. Once there was a final medical exam which the students considered to have been very unfair. One student wrote a letter to the administration on behalf of all of us. He was very nervous about it, that it might have been worded too strongly. But we Germans found it very mild indeed.

Sandeep works in Romandie with colleagues from different countries. He also sees a difference in the communication style of German, French and Swiss colleagues:

My German colleagues are much more structured and organised and straight in telling you what needs to be done. They will not sugar-coat things. This is helpful to make things clear in many areas. My French colleagues have stronger opinions than the French-speaking Swiss, who listen more and are more modest in their opinions. They are not into controversial discussions and try to be more neutral.

The script of matter-of-factness

The interviewees mentioned above describe local people they know as having a mild, modest, unassuming, diplomatic, neutral or understated communication style. This can be contrasted with a more expressive style used in other parts of the world. (Please also see later in this chapter for a discussion of how local people might express criticism more directly.) As an example, Anna Wierzbicka, a Polish linguist, uses the term "script of sincerity" to describe the way people in Poland say and show what they really feel even if the feelings are negative, like "feeling grumpy".[32] She compares this with people in the USA who follow "the smile code". They value cheerfulness, enthusiasm and a genuine state of feeling happy. This is then reflected in their smile. Cheerfulness is often more important than spontaneity or sincerity.

Local employees in Switzerland may not want to draw attention to their feelings or discuss them with their colleagues or clients if they do not know them well. I describe this approach as following a script of "matter-of-factness", known in German as *Sachlichkeit*. People's feelings are personal and private and they don't want to burden the shared emotional space with them. They may express more emotion when they get together with family and friends, on the inside of the coconut.

Crazy emotional people

Theo has British parents and grew up in Switzerland. "I have been accused by foreigners of being cold," he told me. "But if you're very emotional, Swiss people will think you are unstable and crazy. They will lose trust in you. And think you can't think straight."

Theo's comment reminded me of an occasion many years ago when I tried to buy half fare cards for use on public transport for my parents' upcoming two-week visit to Switzerland. The year before, I had bought the cards at the ticket counter at the station and given them to my parents when they arrived at the airport. So, the following year I went to the new travel centre at the station to buy the cards. The assistant there told me I couldn't have them in advance. My parents had to come personally to buy them once they were in the country.

I told him I had bought them in advance at the ticket counter the previous year. "That's not possible," he replied. "Are you saying I'm lying?" I asked in an offended tone. Then he took a step back, and wouldn't discuss it further with me. He obviously thought he was dealing with an unstable and crazy person. I then went to the ticket counter instead and bought the cards just as I had the year before. (I resisted the temptation to go and show them to the unhelpful assistant to prove that I was right.)

In German-speaking Switzerland, many people believe emotions can get in the way of the facts. Employees working with the public are not used to a lot of emotional expression and are often not trained to deal with it. Expressing emotion just weakens your argument as it suggests you can't think clearly any more. This can be contrasted with the point of view of people from more emotionally expressive cultures. For them, you will not sound convincing if you do *not* show emotion. People will assume the matter is not very important. Angelo's boss at the beginning of this chapter may have needed to shout a bit to show his employees that he was serious.

Present the facts

I found it insulting not to be believed by the travel centre assistant, and at the time I found it appropriate to express my anger. However, if I got into that situation now, I would suppress any strong feelings and start to speak slowly and rationally about the facts, and show that the wheels were turning in my brain as I spoke. I would say, "That's strange. I bought them at the ticket counter last year. Have you changed your processes recently?" This approach is also important when dealing with medical emergencies. It is best to present your case as calmly as possible, and provide the facts immediately, no matter how distraught you are. It is advisable not to name the emotion you are feeling, like "I'm so scared." It is more convincing to say, "I think" than "I feel."

It is not just in Switzerland that emotional expression is an issue. Christian Hannig, an intercultural trainer for rescue services in Germany, describes how people from southern European countries are sometimes not taken seriously by German professionals in a medical emergency.[33] It is a vicious circle. If they describe their pain very expressively, complaining loudly and using strong facial expressions, the professionals feel alienated (*befremdet*) and distance themselves, which makes the person in trouble feel misunderstood and even more in need of attention. (This can also be an issue when giving birth.) It is a divide between an "out with it" approach and a "pull yourself together approach" to pain and unpleasant feelings. Hannig emphasises the need for health and emergency professionals to have psychosocial competence that includes intercultural competence.

Getting excited about new ideas

If local people in Switzerland do not express emotion, their colleagues abroad might wrongly think they are not getting on board with new ideas. Markus is a Swiss product development team leader who noticed this:

> I think, we're quite often perceived as not being enthusiastic, as not really buying in, not responding. Our American colleagues get excited about a new idea and say, "Oh yes. This is great. Let's do it!" and in Switzerland we just look at them and think "They don't really mean it. It's just what's expected of them. But it doesn't mean they will now work all night trying to make the thing happen." In Switzerland, if you see people just sitting quietly saying "OK, we'll do that," it means they are really going to do it. But the lack of enthusiasm, the lack of feedback, is puzzling for people in the US. To them it means we are not embracing new things.

In Markus's opinion, his American colleagues seemed to be applying brainstorming techniques to team meetings. One of the rules of brainstorming is that in the first stage, a group should be open to all new ideas suggested spontaneously and greet them positively. (This is similar to the case of Justin exploring the possibility of visiting Mara in Switzerland in Chapter 1.) Local employees in Switzerland may not express much positivity or a "can-do mentality" in response to spontaneous ideas, because this can be seen as carelessness and a lack of forethought. They may find it difficult to say, "yes" immediately to something they haven't had time to think through. If they do respond immediately to a new idea, they may start by suggesting why it might not work. This can be disappointing to people who are enjoying the buzz of thinking of new ideas.

Being corrected

Some incomers are very surprised to hear that local people are described as having a diplomatic communication style. They are probably thinking of a situation where they have been corrected for doing something wrong, as described in Chapter 11 on neighbourhood conflicts. In this chapter I consider the topic in connection with the workplace. Many Swiss are initially surprised to realise how personally incomers take negative feedback, like Nina, a young teacher who is Swiss and Sri Lankan:

> For me the Germans are the most direct people, and the Swiss are the friendly ones who never hurt anybody. But when I talked to people from different cultures, I realised we really are direct. For us, it's nothing special to say what we think, without meaning it personally, but we don't think about the feelings of others when we do that. We don't think that the point in question has something to do with anyone's feelings. It's simply a technical matter.

If the technical matter is something like sending your Swiss colleague some documents by a deadline, and if you don't do it, they may send what seems like a rather pointed reminder, along the lines of "Please send the documents immediately." This may be perceived as an angry tone by a native English speaker while German-speaking Swiss see it as just reminding the person of their duty. It is not meant to be taken personally. A local person who is aware of this as an intercultural communication issue may write, "Could you please send me the documents . . ." and give a reason why they are needed urgently, to avoid sounding angry.

I once attended a meeting of HR managers in Switzerland in connection with a Dutch company taking over a Swiss company. The Dutch head of HR and a Dutch consultant both needed a taxi to get to the airport at the end of the meeting. The Swiss secretary came in and told the consultant, "Your taxi's on its way." The head of HR asked, "Is my taxi on its way too?" "No, you didn't order a taxi," she replied. "Yes, I did," he insisted. "No, you didn't," she repeated, "but I can order you one." He raised his eyebrows, surprised that she was so direct about it. She was focusing on the facts as she saw them and not on his feelings or his position as a senior executive in his company.

Knowledge-based power

When Swiss people correct others, they may be exercising the power that comes from knowledge of the facts, the rules or agreed processes, rather than hierarchical or personal power. For some people from other cultures, any openly-expressed negative feedback can be very threatening. Just the *fact* of being corrected or criticised by people who are not dressed in a police uniform and have no official authority over others can be a bit of a shock.

Where does the tradition of correcting people come from? Switzerland's education system is built on giving people accurate feedback as a pedagogical or didactic device to help them to improve. Nearly 70% of the Swiss population go through the apprenticeship system and many become qualified in skills with high value in the marketplace. They are used to being taught, trying things out, being corrected and improving until they reach the required standard. It is often a straightforward, technical matter and part of the process involves accepting criticism as something neutral and useful. Getting things right is more important than feelings. Later, it may be their responsibility to make sure others do things correctly too.

Feedback in Romandie

People report being corrected more in German-speaking Switzerland than in other parts of the country. Alain is French and has worked as a consultant all over Switzerland. He has experienced this when giving presentations:

> German Swiss may go back over your slides and ask detailed questions. "What do you mean by that?" It's rational thinking. It's good to have perfect slides. If there is a mistake in the date, they will notice and could say something. If you make a presentation in Geneva or Neuchâtel, it is more about the relationship with the client. You might talk for ten minutes about your life, and your weekend. Your presentation should be very enthusiastic, over-selling in a

way, by German-Swiss standards. Even if you only have a few slides, they'll say, "It's really good!"

Indirect criticism

John is an English project team leader who told me about an incident which illustrated his indirect communication style. He described how he wanted Fred, a new member of his team, to join his local colleagues in John's office for a telephone conference with team members abroad. Instead, Fred just joined the call from his own desk in a nearby building. John spoke to him about it when he next saw him:

> Fred came by my office and I said, "Look it would be really nice if you would come along in person. People don't know who you are, because you've normally only been on the phone in these team meetings."

I used this example of indirect communication with international groups and found that some Germans and German-speaking Swiss thought that by saying, "it would be really nice," John was giving Fred the choice as to whether to join the telephone conference in person. They didn't notice a correction or instruction in his comment. Others recognised the polite request as an instruction. Someone said it was not just a technical matter, but could be political, in the sense of office politics. This may also influence whether people phrase things diplomatically. An alternative approach is to say nothing at all, which is common in Swiss meetings when people do not agree with a suggestion. Then there are usually no negative consequences.

Indirect praise

An emphasis on matter-of-factness also has an impact on the praise culture of an organisation. Some incomers experience a general tendency not to praise people at work. This could be connected with the idea that something working well is the norm and you only need to comment if something is wrong. Rick is from the USA and works for a small company in Canton Bern. He told me that he found no encouragement about what he was doing right:

> I was almost starved of feedback in the beginning. I was wondering, "What am I doing well? Where can I focus and improve?" I just got corrections: "This is not enough – didn't you see this problem?" I started to wonder, "Am I making a meaningful contribution to this enterprise?" It was hard until I realised that no feedback means I am doing well and the leadership will let us know if it's not right. The approach to enterprise itself relies on the initiative of staff. They know their responsibilities and fulfil them to the highest level of efficiency and quality they are able to.

I have experienced criticism as positive in Switzerland. I once gave a workshop for the subsidiary of a Swiss company in England. They were very pleased with it and said everyone in their division needed to have my workshop. I never heard from them again. In contrast, I gave a similar workshop in Basel. The head of HR attended and gave me feedback at the end. He told me three things that were wrong with the workshop and then asked, "When can you come again?" What seemed like criticism as a prelude to saying why they wouldn't want me to come back was actually an investment in me. They wanted to improve my workshop to fit their needs.

Local people may give positive feedback in an understated way in Switzerland. They might just say, "Thank you very much," like the HR manager above, if some input is helpful or a job is well done. They do not necessarily put into words what was helpful about it. Being thanked can be valuable feedback.

Chapter 17   Taking up space at work

Chapter 8 explored the topic of how much space we occupy and how we negotiate shared space, both physically and psychologically. This also has an impact on the way people communicate in the workplace, as this chapter explores.

Inviting people to speak

I once participated in a meeting in England to discuss the development of a new product. Various specialists from the company in Switzerland, England, and the USA came to give their input on early stage development. The team leader was English and had never worked in Switzerland. Christian, a quiet Swiss scientist, should have had a contribution to make, but he did not make it. There were some pretty strong characters present and holding forth, and he did not say anything during the whole day of meetings.

At the end of the day, I heard the English team leader say to an English colleague, "I don't know what Christian was doing here. He didn't say a word all day." Why did Christian not contribute to the discussion? It could be that he was not used to contributing in English or that he found it hard to get a word in edgeways in the lively discussions. It might also be, quite simply, that he was used to waiting to be invited by his colleagues to speak.

Swiss groups usually run well without a leader. One aspect of self-regulation in group discussions is that if some people talk too much, and others don't speak, someone will notice this, and invite the quiet ones to speak up. This means you do not have to fight to have your say as you will get your turn eventually. Degrees of introversion are influenced by people's personalities as well as their upbringing and education. In Switzerland, it is more widely accepted to behave as an introvert, like Christian, than in many English-speaking cultures.

Some international team leaders based in Switzerland accept that their teams consist of a mix of talkative and quiet people. They value the contributions of quieter people and take an active role in giving everyone a chance to speak. Peter is a British project leader in a Swiss-based development team involving extroverted and introverted marketing and technical people. He likes it if new members can "jump right in" and start contributing from the start. If they don't manage to do this, and others dominate the discussion, he sees it as his task to manage the situation and coach the quieter people:

> There might be someone who always thinks they've got the right answer, in combination with letting everyone know that. They are very confident, knowledgeable too, which is the scary thing, as people then go, "They're more knowledgeable than me so they must be right." But they're not. There may be better solutions to something, but it takes quieter people in the team to say it. And they are afraid to speak up.

So if this person's on a roll (*talking a lot*), you have to interject, "Okay, thanks. Got your point, thanks very much. So, Sam, what do you reckon about this?" And just be very directive. I would say to the under-talkative person: "I know you may not feel too comfortable sometimes, but you've got a lot to contribute, I'd really like you to do that, because I'd like the team to hear what you've got to say". I want them to talk, actually, for their own development.

Thoughtful and wise

Quiet people are often seen as thoughtful and wise in Swiss groups. This contrasts with attitudes reported in the USA. In her book on introversion, *Quiet*, American author Susan Cain comments that people who speak more are considered more intelligent, more likable, and better leaders.[34] In addition, quick talkers are rated as more capable and appealing than slow talkers. She concludes, however, by saying that, according to research, more talking is not correlated with greater insight. She suggests that something might be wrong with a leadership style that values quick and assertive answers over quiet, slow decision-making. Peter, the project leader, would agree with her on this.

Susan Cain gives the example of university students role-playing a "Subarctic Survival Situation". Working in teams, the students had to choose fifteen items and rank them in order of importance to a group's survival. In one team a young man had extensive experience in the northern backwoods and quietly expressed his views about how to rank the items. But his group didn't listen and chose ideas suggested by the most vocal people in the group.

I imagine his ideas would have been more heard and appreciated in a Swiss team.

Interrupting

Without a leader like Peter to facilitate the discussion, members of a lively group may need to interrupt other people who are talking too much. In English classes on holding meetings, students are even taught a range of expressions to "interrupt politely", as interrupting is assumed to be the norm. This does not work so well in German. In conversations, a German-speaking Swiss person's "turn" is likely to have a clear beginning, middle and end, as in "A + B + C". It has to be a grammatically complete utterance because if you interrupt before they have finished, you might miss "C", the most important verb at the end of the sentence. In English and in other languages, you might have a circular argument, saying a little bit about A, then B, then C, then back to A again. It can be acceptable to hold the floor until someone stops you. Once someone has got your point, they can come in with their view.

Karin is from Cologne in Germany and sees a different approach in the communication styles of Swiss people, whether they are speaking English or German:

> When Swiss people talk, the speed is different. They are much calmer, and pause more often. When they do, you shouldn't jump in and start talking. I notice a difference compared to my own experience from the Rhine region of Germany. We talk about something, and when we're finished, we expect the other person to

immediately start talking. Like playing tennis, back and forward. If they don't, we start talking again. There mustn't be a communication gap.

For me it is also normal to interrupt someone to complete their sentence for them. You are showing them, "I know what you mean, I understand you." When I do this with Swiss people, they are shocked and stop talking. There is also a difference with regard to warming up. In Switzerland you chat a bit before you get to the point. It is more efficient in the end because you win the other person's trust.

Interrupting is seen by some Swiss people as a really bad habit. If you see a conversation like a game of golf, rather than tennis, it is like getting your golf club tangled with the other person's before they have finished their shot. And their shot may take a while, once they get going. It is not like a tennis volley, where the ball goes back and forward quickly between the two players. I once observed an assessment centre exercise run by a Swiss company in order to identify employees with leadership potential. Six participants from different countries had to discuss a problem, and the Swiss facilitator observed us to see who showed the most leadership in the discussion.

In the debrief he told a South African participant. "You interrupted several times." I did not find interrupting so bad, especially as some of the candidates were going to be working in London and would need the skill of interrupting to get their ideas across in meetings in the city.

Sarah is Swiss and comments that English speakers are too impatient. We just can't sit out a moment of silence. Swiss people take a moment to think about what has just been said. Again, it is like playing golf. You can wait a moment after the other person has hit their ball, before you hit yours.

Learning to listen
Swiss children learn listening skills at school. According to education experts Peter Sieber and Horst Sitta, this involves listening, letting others talk and being silent. Being silent in company is a high form of the capacity for intimate communication.[35] They call it the "being" dimension of communication ability. It could be seen as similar to the white space in a Swiss advertisement in a glossy magazine. It does not need to be filled. In comparison, from a Swiss perspective, some foreign advertisements seem to be very "busy", communicating lots of different messages at the same time.

Silence as a sales strategy

People in Switzerland sometimes use the word "influence" to complain about people behaving in an overpowering way. "She tried to influence me," they will comment. Influencing implies entering someone's private brain space and trying to change their thinking. It is a form of interfering with the person. English-speaking readers may find it far-fetched that you can interact with others, exchange ideas and then make decisions without being influenced by them. "Of course they are being influenced," they will say. "They just don't realise it."

I argue that people in Switzerland sometimes try to influence each other by being silent. Anyone who has been left to think quietly while standing next to both a beautiful new car and a car salesman (and it is usually a man) in a Swiss car showroom will appreciate this technique. He presents the facts and technical data about the car, then backs off to let you think about it. This tells you that the facts about this car speak for themselves, and with a bit of logic and rational thought, you will come to the right conclusion about it.

You can attribute all kinds of things to a silent salesperson, like depth of character, wisdom, appreciation for the good things in life, and of course, most importantly, the compliment paid by the confidence he has in your judgment that you will make the right decision without his interference. If you come from a country where sales people give it the hard sell, you might be a bit uneasy at this lack of effort. In Switzerland this quiet attentiveness is extremely convincing.

Don't "big yourself up"

You can take up space with the way you talk about yourself. It is difficult to get a good balance in this area in an international workplace. In a course I gave for a Swiss company in the USA, I met Heather, an American HR manager who had also worked in Switzerland. She explained the problem they had trying to align Swiss and American ways of presenting achievements:

My American co-worker described in an email to Switzerland how far his team were with their project. He wrote: "We have completed an awesome 186 pages." I told him not to write that. It's too much in Switzerland. You don't big yourself up when you've done something worthy of praise. You should just state baldly that you or a member of your team has done it. Saying "Harriet has created a spreadsheet to show us the results" is enough, not "Harriet has done an amazing job creating a spreadsheet." This is also a problem when writing an employee assessment. An assessment written by an American could be very positive and the person could be seen as an exceptional employee by a Swiss reader.

Networking and one-upmanship

The issue of whether and how to present your achievements is relevant to the way you go about networking. Networking is a good way to increase your visibility, but it might need to be done modestly with local people. Jantien is Dutch and has worked in Switzerland for many years. She experiences a different approach to networking, depending on the nationality of the people she networks with:

> In all cases, my aim is to build a trusting relationship. So if I am networking with international people at work, if I've initiated having a coffee with them, I will tell them about the paper on project management that I have been writing for my part-time MBA. Then they will say, "Oh, really? How would you apply that to our setting?" Internationals chat over coffee about business – this launch, and that project – and demonstrate their know-how in a very chatty manner.

When she is having coffee with local Swiss or German colleagues, Jantien finds it important to avoid what could be seen as one-upmanship:

> Swiss people do not really want to hear me telling them about my expertise if it is not a job interview and they don't have a vacant position. If I contacted a Swiss colleague ostensibly just for a

coffee, and started to tell them about my vast knowledge of project management, they would just look at me and wouldn't take me up on the subject. Germans would also find it inappropriate.

Instead I ask them where they live and talk about where I live. We discuss where they're going on holiday and where they like to have lunch or I tell them about a wine tasting I went to. If they have children we will both talk about our children. After we've solidly covered a lot of general ground, I might ask them a question about their business near the end of our chat.

If I wish to network with a Swiss or German person on a higher level than me, I approach them with a business question and ask them to have coffee with me. Perhaps I'd like to hear more about the direction of a new project they are responsible for that will impact on my team. We'll chat generally for ten minutes, and then turn to the business question. I listen to what they have to say, and only subtly hint at my own commitment or expertise in the matter. Perhaps I can make a comment about how seriously I and my team are taking the milestones on their new project.

Part five: Studying in Switzerland

Chapter 18 Classroom dynamics

This section of the book is specifically for people coming from abroad to study at a Swiss university.[36] If you are interested in knowing more about Swiss schooling at kindergarten, primary or secondary level, please see "Going Local – your guide to Swiss schooling".[37]

Various topics covered in this book are relevant to student life in Switzerland, from keeping to arrangements and being punctual in Part One to understanding attitudes to relationships in Part Two. This chapter addresses aspects of teaching styles and classroom dynamics that overlap with some topics in Part Four, such as participative decision-making, attitudes to hierarchy and self-directed employees.

Participating in class

Irene is Spanish and is studying in Switzerland for a master's degree. She was enrolled as a bachelor's student of business administration in Madrid when she first spent a year abroad in Switzerland as an exchange student. She noticed that the students at her university of applied sciences in Switzerland had closer contact with lecturers and staff than in Spain:

In Madrid everything is on such a large scale, you are just a number. The lecturers probably never knew my name. In Switzerland the lecturers and staff are very accessible and supportive. They know people and try to find solutions for them. The local students are also more actively involved, organising events for everyone, being a buddy to exchange students, and even picking people up at the airport.

Irene also described the teaching style at her Swiss university as more communicative:

In Spain there are two different types of classes, the theoretical input with around 90 students in an auditorium and the smaller classes of 30 with a practical focus, where the students are supposed to have closer contact with the lecturer. In the theory classes in Spain, you try to sit up the back, as far away as possible from the lecturer. In the practical classes, if you have to sit near the front, you try and take cover behind the people in the front row, so that you won't be asked to speak. In Switzerland a class typically has 30–40 students and they like being in the first row and are always putting up their hands. Some love to debate with the lecturer and disagree openly with each other.

Nicole was one of a group of students from France spending a year at a Swiss university of applied sciences. She found it difficult that lecturers in Switzerland seek to enter into a dialogue with students. "They are on the same level as the students. They ask them questions and encourage them to reflect on their views. If a lecturer asks me something, my mind goes blank." Michel, her French classmate, explained why it was surprising:

In France you have a very "high hierarchy" and you are only a student. The teacher tells us the truth and we will accept it. Here in

Switzerland the teacher doesn't tell us the truth. He gives us a text and asks us to build an opinion and then argue with him about it. But we are not used to arguing with the teacher.

Questioning the lecturer

As Irene and Michel noticed, local students in Switzerland love to debate with their lecturers. It is part of the Swiss understanding of direct democracy that people with power have to be accessible and answerable to others, and defend their views and decisions. It is reminiscent of a transactional style of leadership, as discussed in Chapter 14 of this book. Some local students have experience from their schooldays of trying to renegotiate their marks. "Can I not get at least half a point for this answer? It's nearly right," they might argue. While studying in France, Mirjam, a Swiss student, was not happy with her group's mark for their presentation in class, because she thought they had done better than another group:

I didn't understand the problem. I just ask the teacher, "Could you please explain to me why you are giving us this mark?", and "Compared with the other group, I don't see why you gave me such a low mark." You can't do this in France. When Swiss students did it, the French students told us, "You are so rude. You don't have manners. You don't behave." For us it was, like, just normal, we had been doing that since primary school.

Lecturers may give students their marks for presentations during class time, but it is increasingly the case that they have to hand marks in to the examination secretary's office instead. Students then have to make an appointment to inspect their mark sheets and marked papers. If they have a complaint, it is handled in an official process. There should be no correspondence with the lecturer.

Mature Swiss students

Swiss students tend to be older than international students, no matter which type of school they previously attended. Around 20% of school pupils complete *Gymnasium*, or academic upper secondary school with a general leaving certificate known, significantly, as a *Matura*, meaning "maturity". Many of these go on to traditional Swiss universities. They are on average around 20 years old when they start.

Nearly 70% of school pupils go on to do an apprenticeship instead of *Gymnasium*. From around the age of 15 to 19, they attend classes and learn professional and social skills in the workplace. Around a quarter of these obtain a *Matura* in their field and many then go on to study at a university of applied sciences. They are on average 23 years old. Some work full-time for a few years first, before they go on to take up their studies.

Giving presentations

Michel experienced that students in Switzerland had to work on case studies in groups. This was usually followed by a presentation to the class of the group's conclusions. In some cases, a mark was given for the presentation. Giving presentations for an individual or group mark (or a combination of the two) may be an integral part of your studies at a Swiss university. You may have to hand in a group paper or sit an exam as well to pass the class in question. As Michel describes, some lecturers also use student presentations as a way to introduce content to the class. Some students from abroad find it odd to be taught in this way by their colleagues instead of the lecturer.

Michel noticed that the local students found presenting easier than the French students:

> I think for me it is part of the Swiss culture, this self-confidence they are really able to stand up in front of the class and speak convincingly. It is quite natural for them. They are older and more experienced than the young French students, who are a little bit shy, who haven't worked before the course.

Local Swiss students are indeed used to presenting. Some even started learning this skill in primary school. I remember my daughter making her first presentation at the age of eight, clutching a set of hand-written cards with just a few words written on each card. Other students have had a lot of work experience, which could include making presentations in their companies. Theo comments that they tend to present very honestly and factually, but not very passionately. They will not try to sell you something.

Distributing group tasks

When it comes to group work, Irene sees the previous work experience of local students as beneficial to exchange students:

> I think that exchange students learn a different approach to education, maybe more applied to real cases, when they work together in teams with local students. Normally, local students are a bit older and have previous working experience. In my case, as an exchange student coming from a traditional university where courses were very theoretical, this particular difference of learning from the experience of classmates was very striking.

Swiss groups like to distribute their work equally, and everyone in the group is normally expected to present. It may be that some group members have never had to present at school or university in their own language, and may feel unable to do so in English. Theo suggests that the group should then work to their set of strengths. "Ask these students what kind of stuff they like doing. In Hong Kong we divided the labour. I did the presentation with fun slides, and the others got behind the books and brought the data. It worked really well."

Lecturers may insist on all students presenting if they are giving them a mark for their presentation, or because they see it as a business skill that they will need in the workplace. Nicole was horrified at the idea of presenting in English at the beginning of her year in Switzerland. At the end of the year she was happy to report that it wasn't a problem any longer. "I've learnt to be self-confident and to speak in front of the class."

Self-regulating groups

Problems may arise when students are doing group work and making a presentation or writing a paper for a mark. Working styles can be different, and students from different countries may find they have different expectations when working together. Swiss students tend to be very experienced in group work and their groups are usually self-regulating, similar to self-directed employees, as discussed in Chapters 14 and 15. They may see it as unnecessary to appoint a leader. They just trust everyone to be motivated and get on with the job. Theo comments that local students really like the Swiss image that they'll be on time without being reminded and that the quality will be good. "It's like a label that you're reliable. Although you do get free riders." (*Trittbrettfahrer* in German)

Speaking to students from different countries, I have often heard them refer to having a group leader or even a manager. Remo is a Swiss student who experienced group work with a Mexican classmate in the role of manager:

> The way our manager handled things was quite extraordinary. She was very responsible and she didn't trust people to do a good job, so it was not like I expected. I would have done it the other way around I would have thought, 'Well people will surely do a good job" and I wouldn't be nervous. She was really nervous and she thought, "They're going to let me down."

Appointing a facilitator

Theo commented that certain personalities will drive the content in group work and two or three people may drive it in different directions. He sees appointing a leader or manager as a "safe" suggestion, but not necessarily the most exciting and rewarding approach:

> It can be a beautiful thing to experience if semi-assertive people from various countries contribute and work together on a project. "May the best idea win" sort of thing. It's important to be able to go through the process of everyone contributing and people saying, "That is a fantastic idea," or "Your first idea was rubbish but I liked your second idea."

Like Theo, many Swiss students prefer not to have someone who gets to make key decisions on the project content. They don't want to be "bossed around" by someone. They would find it more acceptable to have a facilitator (often referred to as a "moderator"), or process leader. This person's main role is to make sure everyone gets a chance to share their ideas and that everyone delivers on time. They would only be assertive about milestones: "Shall we agree to have all our data collection done by next Monday? Can everyone manage that?" They will also remind people of deadlines: "Just to remind you, everyone has to have their slides ready by Thursday."

Having a facilitator can also be a solution to the "freerider" problem, which can affect any group. A few local students may be overextended with work and private commitments and will not do their share of the work. Incoming students may be travelling a lot, or returning regularly to their home country. Swiss groups will not report it to the lecturer if someone is not pulling their weight. It is a custom from their schooldays that you do not "tell tales". As Theo puts it, "You are responsible to each other, and no matter how inefficient your colleagues are it is still your group." A facilitator can encourage people to decide their workload and deadlines together, and draw in the underperforming team member, whether local or from abroad.

Chapter 19 Socialising with local students

Buddy programmes

Rosa is from Mexico and previously studied in Mexico and Australia. I spoke to her while she was studying on one of the many bachelors' and masters' programmes now available in English around Switzerland. She was disappointed that she had not managed to get to know the local Swiss students on her international programme better but was pleased to have made friends among the international students like herself.

"In Mexico we were quite open to the internationals, asking if they needed advice," she told me. "We organised parties with them and took them to places to help them get to know people." In Australia she was also welcomed by the locals. "Everyone in the class said where they were from and at the break the Australians came to introduce themselves to the visiting students. They wanted to work with us in teams."

As it happened, the Swiss students were in the minority in Rosa's class in Switzerland, and the few local students would have had their work cut out initiating a friendship with the many international students. It is also typical that Swiss students are busy with their own lives and do not make time for new relationships, unless it is formalised in some way. More will be said about this later. (See also Chapter 5 on peaches and coconuts.) From my conversations with students who have studied abroad, it varies greatly around the world as to whether there is a warm welcome awaiting exchange students, or whether they are left to their own devices.

Universities in Switzerland are increasingly proactive in encouraging mixing between local and international students. At my university, introduction weeks with welcome sessions and buddy programmes are organised for incoming students, to help them get their bearings and settle into life in Switzerland.[38] Local students, or "buddies", organise activities, events and outings for the incomers. They go shopping with them and take them home to meet their families.

Alexandra works with international students and told me the story of a male Brazilian student who transferred over to being a local student at her university. He was the buddy of a female Swiss student. When she moved out of her mother's house, he moved in.

Theo Whitwill is the president of the Erasmus Student Network in Switzerland. He sees it as important to have a structured buddy programme:

> A lot of students don't see the big picture at first. It is a privilege to be able to go abroad and be welcomed by another university. But for me to go abroad there needs to be a "me" who comes here. If incoming students feel isolated, they are not going to tell others to come here. Our students need a push to become a buddy so we frame it as a duty to contribute. Some students come back from their semester abroad a bit changed. They enjoyed the buddy

system abroad and want to give something back. Some even become the buddies of four different people.

Coconut universities
Local students in Switzerland may not be the easiest demographic group for incomers to get to know. Many students are still deeply connected with the communities of their childhood. They have busy lives, juggling their studies and possibly working part-time, as well as seeing their family and keeping up with their friends from their teenage years.

The Swiss government even has a policy of building new universities of applied sciences (and the new buildings of the more traditional universities) right next to the train stations of Swiss cities to encourage students to travel daily from other cities and cantons. Public transport is excellent, and if they are studying in another city, they may travel back home every evening, or at least most weekends. There is often no campus life to speak of. This all supports a "coconut" style culture, helping people to continue their life as it was before. It makes buddy programmes very important.

Swiss students who are interested in getting to know people from other countries are likely to study or travel abroad to experience a different culture and the people in it. As Theo mentions, they often befriend international students when they come back. One of the changes students may experience is the way they see relationships with new people. Léonie is from Romandie and describes how she feels about the Swiss "coconut style "respect for privacy" and "waiting for incomers to signal that they want contact", mentioned in Chapter 10:

> My best experience was two years ago, when I was abroad for two months: I had the possibility to speak with people from the whole world and I really had the time to get to know them better. When I'm travelling, I realise how good I feel: I feel free to ask or speak with someone, even if people don't speak my native language. In Switzerland, due to this respect for privacy, I'm afraid of acting like that.
>
> This respect for privacy is quite complex. On one hand, I think that it's a positive thing because it means that I'm respectful and I don't want to disturb people. But on the other hand, it makes me feel uncomfortable because sometimes I would like to speak with someone, but I don't dare. With this high value placed on independence, we prefer generally to stay silent, waiting for "the signal". That's a shame, because if everyone is waiting for the signal, then nobody will speak.

The good news is that, even without buddy programmes, increasing numbers of Swiss students are spending a semester abroad and get used to initiating interactions with relative strangers. Some may have started learning an additional foreign language (after French/German/Italian and English), such as Chinese or Spanish, and may see it as a good opportunity to practise with incoming students. It is worth "giving the signal", as Léonie mentions, and showing local people that you are interested in them and their travels abroad.

Job-seeking strategies

Some incomers to Switzerland who do not yet have a job here consider studying at a Swiss university as a way in, to build their local network and find work. This can be a good strategy if the university programme also explicitly offers work placements or if there is a buddy programme. However, if you are already well-qualified, you might gain more from taking an intensive course in the local language, so that you can apply for local jobs. Then you will also be better able to communicate with local people in their language, and participate fully in local activities. This can also lead to job opportunities, as the local people you know may tell you when a job is going in their workplace. In German-speaking Swiss workplaces an additional challenge may be that local people speak to each other in Swiss German. This topic is discussed in Part Six of the book.

A good reference

It is worth noting that a good reference from a Swiss employer is very valuable, and that it can pay off to take a lower level, part-time or temporary job as a contractor in the field you are interested in. This will give you initial work experience and a reference in the local setting. Swiss references are a formal matter, and are signed off by the HR department of companies. Being able to provide a good reference from a known local company may reduce some of the uncertainty involved in hiring you for the next employer.

Part six: The Swiss German challenge

Chapter 20 Understanding Swiss German

If you plan to settle in Switzerland, you will probably want to start learning the local language where you live. In French and Italian-speaking Switzerland this is relatively straightforward. The language you learn in a language school, online, or in self-study will be more or less the same as the language spoken by local people in your neighbourhood and at work. In the German-speaking part of the country, however, this is quite different. Most people who grew up there speak a dialect, and it is quite different from the High German you will learn in a German class or in self-study. This chapter and the following one address this issue.

The goat on the mountain

Seventy employees from an international company met at their Swiss headquarters for a training seminar. Many flew in from the USA and China. One evening they took a quiz on their knowledge of Swiss German, prepared by local employees from Basel. (The quiz can be found on pages 185–186.)

The quiz was light-hearted, confirming the usual clichés about Switzerland as the country where people live in the mountains and yodel and milk their goats, just like in Heidi, the famous children's book. Chinese employees asked their Swiss colleagues to sing the goat song and say the tongue twister in Section C of the quiz, and they duly obliged. It also led to a discussion on Swiss German dialect. The German-speaking Swiss employees explained that they always spoke Swiss German dialect among themselves, not just to sing traditional songs, but also in business meetings, for example, to talk about project milestones or their new training handbook.

Dialect stigma

Newcomers from western English-speaking countries are often surprised to hear that people would speak in a dialect in a business meeting in Switzerland, as dialects are somewhat stigmatised and seen as a substandard version of English. As a child in Scotland, I had to attend weekly elocution classes from the age of three, to iron out my strong Scottish accent (and any non-standard grammar) and make me understandable to English people, or so my mother said. Many of the girls liked going to "elocution", but some of the boys hated it and nicknamed it "execution".

In Germany, dialect also has lower status than in Switzerland, especially in the north. While in Bavaria, 45% of the population say they speak dialect all the time, in northern Germany, only 10% say this.[39] A few people there speak it at home, but it is rarely spoken outside the home. In German-speaking Switzerland, dialect is spoken as much as possible by more or less 100% of the people who grew up there. It has nothing to do with people's level of education. Put very simply, Swiss German is their first language. High German is the language they learn to understand as pre-schoolers by watching children's programmes on TV or on YouTube. They learn to speak and write it at the latest when they start school. They continue to speak Swiss German as the language of their childhood, all their lives. Nowadays many people write it too, in social media or in text messages.

High German or Standard German
Educationalists and academics correctly refer to High German or *Hochdeutsch* as "Standard German". Put simply, the word "high" was originally used to distinguish this form of German from the "Low German" of northern Germany. I use "High German" in this book as it is the term most commonly used by local people.

Many German-speaking Swiss feel that High German is their first foreign language that they speak very well, but do not feel completely at home in. Some are self-conscious about making mistakes in it. They may make an effort to speak High German with learners who do not understand dialect, but they try to avoid speaking it to each other. If you are learning to speak High German in Switzerland, you will hear people speaking Swiss German too. In this chapter, I show some examples of how this works in practice.

Swiss German quiz

(The answers can be found in the appendix on page 204.)

Section A: Vocabulary

Choose the correct translation of these words.

1. Flugzüg
   a) Escape
   b) Airplane
   c) Flu
   d) Fluctuation

2. Chuchichäschtli
   a) Kitchen cupboard
   b) Cheese pie
   c) Lollipop
   d) Shoe cupboard

3. Poschte
   a) Post office
   b) Lamp post
   c) Shopping
   d) Tram

Section B: Reading

Read this Swiss German song and indicate if the statements below are true or false.

Det äne am Bergli, det schtat e wissy Geiss.
I ha si welle mälche, da haut si mer eis.
Holeduli, duliduli, holeduliduliduli,
holeduli, duliduli, holeduliduldulio.

	True	False
1. The goat is brown.		
2. The goat is standing on the mountain.		
3. The narrator was hit by the goat.		
4. The narrator hit the goat back.		

Section C: Speaking

You may practice this tongue twister now:
De Pabscht hät z'Spiez s'Späck-Bschteck zspot bschtellt.
(Translation: The pope ordered the bacon cutlery too late in Spiez)

© *The New Beyond Chocolate – Understanding Swiss Culture*,
by Margaret Oertig, Bergli Books, 2019.

Ka, ka, ka

"At first I only understood *ka, ka, ka i*n Swiss German," said Alison, a British mother who lives in the Basel region. She speaks High German when she is talking one-to-one with local people and English with her children and her Swiss boyfriend, Dani. Her children go to local school and speak Swiss German with Dani and his parents. Alison and her children also have lunch regularly with other families in the neighbourhood. Then everyone except Alison speaks Swiss German. She finds it hard to follow what they are saying to each other. "I tell them to speak dialect because I want them to be able to speak naturally," she told me. "It's a pity if they have to speak High German because of me."

Alison often gets lost in conversations in Swiss German. A neighbour explained to her that the *ka, ka, ka* she kept hearing was actually the Basel dialect word *gha*, which means *had*, as in *I have had lunch*. It sounds quite different from the High German word *gehabt*. She has decided to start learning Swiss German, to be able to understand the conversations going on around her.

Double Dutch

I first encountered Swiss German in the language school in England where I taught English to adults from all over the world, including many German-speaking Swiss. I already spoke High German and Dutch, but was surprised at how little I understood of the different Swiss German dialects I overheard. I was used to listening in and picking up the basics of new languages, but with Swiss German, not much was sticking.

After eight months in the school I visited Switzerland for Christmas with Hans, my future husband. In my linguistic rucksack I had a random set of words I had picked up from my students: *ig, chlii, glii, e bitzeli, Schoggi* and *gell*.[40] *Gell* seemed to be particularly important. It means "isn't it?" (*nicht wahr?*), and Anita, a student from Zurich, always said it at the end of her sentences in English.

In Switzerland that Christmas I had no idea what Hans' family were saying to each in Swiss German. In contrast, their High

German was easy enough to understand because they spoke it fairly slowly and clearly, like a foreign language they were very fluent in.

I experienced Swiss German and High German as two related but different languages. (The correct linguistic term would be two different "varieties".) As I understood it in the language school in England and on that first visit to Switzerland, I could speak one language reasonably well (High German), but was a beginner in the other language (Swiss German). It may be partly because I was hearing different dialects all the time, and people were using different words to express the same thing. Even the word for "I" could be *i*, *ich* or *ig*.

Swiss German at work

Alison had attended High German classes for many years as an investment in her future. She thought she might need it one day when she was looking for a new job. Marieke is a nurse from the Netherlands who was also learning High German in order to find work in Switzerland. Once she had reached an intermediate level (B1), she was offered a job in a hospital in the east of Switzerland. It was to her advantage that she was looking after patients in single rooms. They became her teachers.

At first patients automatically spoke Swiss German to Marieke, but when they noticed she didn't understand they changed to High German. They also took the time to explain dialect words that she did not know yet. When a patient said, "Could you pass me my slippers?" she used the dialect word *Finken* for slippers, which means "finches" in High German. Marieke started looking round for birds in a cage, and wondered why the patient wanted to take them to the toilet with her.

Some patients were very ill and reverted to dialect. In the early days, a colleague translated for Marieke and with time she learned to understand a lot. She also had to learn to understand her colleagues speaking to her in a range of different Swiss German dialects, from the cantons of St Gallen, Thurgau and Appenzell. Some of them changed to High German when she said she didn't understand, while others continued to speak their dialect, just more slowly.

The team leader held team meetings in High German until Marieke got used to Swiss German. After two years, Marieke could understand what was being said in dialect in a structured meeting situation where the team leader was giving a lot of predictable information and instructions. However, she still could not understand the informal chats in different dialects at the *Znüni Pause*, the morning coffee break. "When eight people are all speaking their different dialects, I just can't follow them. I often ask someone afterwards what they were talking about." Marieke continues to learn and speak High German as the standard language.

Camilla is from Sweden and was advised to take a different approach at work. Like Marieke, she had been learning High German and found a job in a hospital laboratory. On the first day, her boss said, "I'm only going to speak Swiss German to you. That's what we speak here and you need to learn it." It made sense to Camilla. "You have to be able to understand if someone orders blood from our laboratory in Swiss German, using the intercom system. You can't afford to make mistakes."

Instead of continuing to improve her High German, Camilla signed up for a Swiss German course locally and started to speak Swiss German at work. Words like *öppis* are very difficult," she explained. (*Öppis* means *etwas or* "something" in High German). "It helps to see how they are written." She later went on to improve her High German too, because she wanted to be able to write it well.

> ### *Baustellendeutsch*
> Many incomers to German speaking Switzerland get jobs in shops, restaurants, production sites and building sites, and learn mainly Swiss German on the job, the way they hear it around them. Some will also go to High German language classes. They may end up speaking a mix of the two. There is even a term *Baustellendeutsch* ("building site German") to refer to this mix.

High German at work

Marieke and Camilla's experience is by no means universal, and in many workplaces people will consistently speak High German to learners. There are also many Germans around who always speak High German, and this helps promote its use at work. Patrick is French and reports how it is done in his traditional Swiss company:

> When I didn't understand Swiss German, they would switch to High German so that I would know what's going on. If someone

spoke Swiss German, another one would say, "*Bitte Hochdeutsch*" ("High German, please"). They are pleased that I can now understand Swiss German. They speak Swiss German to me and I reply in High German. It is important to write it in your CV if you understand Swiss German. People appreciate that.

Learning good High German *and* learning to understand Swiss German can be a very intensive long-term project, but can reap rewards. Uli came to Switzerland as an expat from Mexico. He attended intensive courses in High German, at 7.30 am, five days a week, for around five years. He then started to apply himself to learning Swiss German. Now, ten years later, he is attending High German courses in writing formal correspondence and leading negotiations in German.

Uli's approach is not possible for everyone, but his ability to speak and understand both languages has given him a high degree of local integration and flexibility in the job market. He originally spoke English in his job in an international company and later changed to a smaller Swiss company where he needs to write email in High German and also understand spoken Swiss German. His new job gives him the opportunity to travel to his home country of Mexico on business, which is an added benefit.

Baby language
Most Germans and Austrians do not learn to speak Swiss German, but instead aim just to understand it. Christoph is Austrian and finds this important, in order to feel part of things:

> After so many years in Switzerland I feel uncomfortable if people speak Swiss German to each other but High German to me. They mean well, but it gives me a feeling of being different. I feel like the toddler whose parents are talking normally to each other and then in a special baby language to me. I don't feel part of the group. The conversation also slows down as they can express themselves better in dialect. So I ask them to speak Swiss German to me.

The stories highlighted in this chapter show where the Swiss German challenge lies. Swiss German speakers find their mother tongue the most natural way to talk each other in all situations. (In linguistic terms, this is a situation of diglossia, where two different varieties of a language are spoken by all the people in a speech community.) They might use High German in formal situations, like a lecture, or to read a written text aloud. If everyone understands Swiss German, they will chat to each other, hold meetings, make presentations and conduct parents' evenings at school in dialect. It is generally accepted that if there are people present who do not speak Swiss German, everyone should change to High German. More is said about this in in the next chapter.

Chapter 21   Learning "the language"

Starting with High German

It is recommended that incomers learn "the language", meaning High German, when they settle in German-speaking Switzerland. Language schools offer a wide range of High German classes. Once you can speak and understand High German, you will start to understand quite a lot of Swiss German too. "90% of the grammar of High German and Swiss German is the same," commented Dominique Serena, director of *Swissing*, a language school in Zurich that offers courses in Swiss German. Several people told me that learning some High German before they came to Switzerland got them off to a good start. An intensive course in your home country or in Germany is a very efficient way to learn without the distraction of hearing Swiss German in the local community or workplace.

Swiss High German

If you are learning High German in Switzerland, you will be taught the local Swiss variety of High German, which is different from the High German of Germany. Many Germans do not know about this difference, which can lead to amusing misunderstandings.

Hans tells the story of an occasion when he was skiing in the Swiss mountain. He chatted to a northern German woman in the ski lift and did his best to speak correct High German, as he had learned it at school. When they got out of the ski lift, she said, "Swiss German is not that difficult. I understood nearly everything you said." Almost all German-speaking Swiss have a story like this. They speak their best High German, and Germans, hearing their accent and some different vocabulary, think that is what Swiss German sounds like.

Some incomers from German-speaking countries think I am joking when I talk about Swiss High German. They tend to think of High German words in Switzerland as cute or just plain wrong if they are different from the High German of Germany. In contrast, few people think American English is correct and British English is cute or wrong, or vice versa. Should you say "sidewalk" or "pavement"? These are different ways of saying the same thing in Standard English in the English-speaking world. This is the case with German too. *Gehsteig* and *Trottoir* (meaning pavement) are both Standard German in Germany and Switzerland respectively.

Grammar can vary too in Swiss High German and Austrian High German. As a simple example, yogurt changes sex when it crosses the border. In Switzerland you say *das Joghurt*, in Germany *der Joghurt* and in Austria either *das Joghurt* or *die Joghurt*.

A Swiss High German dictionary
A good way to get an overview of official Swiss High German words is to have a look through the "Duden Schweizerhochdeutsch", a slim Duden dictionary for Swiss High German which

lists around 3000 words used in the High German of Switzerland.[41] (There is also a Duden for Austrian German.) If you use these words, you will be showing your geographical identity, as you will be speaking High German with a local flavour. Another advantage of learning some of these Swiss High German terms is that many of them are also used in Swiss German dialect.

"Keep complaining"

When you learn High German as one of the national languages (in German: *Landessprachen*) of Switzerland you will be in good company. In Romandie and Ticino, people learn High German as an official Swiss language at school, and many have difficulty understanding Swiss German dialect. In Romandie, some people call High German "proper" German (*le bon allemand*, literally "good German"). They are often assertive about asking people to speak "proper German" to them. Linguists from Fribourg University recommend the following in a book about Swiss German:[42]

If you have problems understanding dialect, say so as soon as possible. This is not impolite. If you do not react, German-speaking Swiss will think you understand dialect. So, especially in the beginning, keep complaining (*immer wieder reklamieren*): "Excuse me, unfortunately I don't understand Swiss German."

You may need to take the linguists' advice if you find yourself in a meeting situation at work or a parents' evening. Very often, the first speaker asks (in Swiss German) if everyone understands Swiss German. You have to listen for the word *Schwyzerdütsch* and be ready to put up your hand immediately and ask the speaker to change to High German. This is accepted as your right.

You may need to put up your hand again later on if another speaker forgets to speak High German. Just seeing you with your hand up will probably remind them immediately to switch back. My German colleague Holger pointed out that speaking Swiss German is often the default position and that you just have to "flick the switch" by saying you don't understand.

How Swiss German and High German are used

You need High German to . . .	You need Swiss German to . . .
• talk to people who don't understand Swiss German • read instruction manuals and labels on products in shops • read and fill in official documents • read letters from your children's teachers • write formal letters • write email to colleagues • read newspapers, websites and books • understand films and some TV and radio programmes	• understand when local people talk to each other, even in your own family • understand local people who won't speak High German to you • talk to children and follow their conversations with each other • understand games, plays and songs at your children's school events • read and write texts and chat messages, e.g. in WhatsApp and social media • understand some TV and radio programmes

Choosing the language to learn

It is most typical that incomers start by learning High German. However, you may have reason to learn Swiss German too, for example, to follow your work colleague's verbal instructions, as Camilla needs to do. Like Alison, you may also want to be able to join in conversations with family members or local people talking to each other, or understand what your children and their friends are saying to each other. The table on page 196 shows you what you can do with High German and Swiss German.

One language at a time, please

Whether you have a greater need to learn High German or Swiss German, it makes sense to focus on only one of the two languages or varieties at a time. After all, if you wanted to learn both Dutch and German, or Norwegian and Swedish, you would start with one, and when you had a good grasp of it, you would then start the other one. It is easier to learn the one that people around you will be willing to practise with you.

Some people even choose to learn Swiss German first, like Jen, an Australian who married a Swiss man from Basel. She speaks Swiss German fluently, but can hardly speak any High German. She learned German for four years at school but could not speak it properly when she came to Switzerland. She talked to her husband about what language they should speak together:

> My husband said High German was a foreign language for him, and we realised that if we spoke English together it wouldn't help

me either. Then I said, 'You know what? I want to communicate with people. I'm not interested in writing.' So I spent the next two years listening to people speaking Swiss German and trying to copy them.

Personality plays a role in the decision regarding which language to learn. Extroverts like me get their energy from interactions with other people. I started to listen and put the puzzle pieces together to build a language out of them. The breakthrough came when I finally understood what *gsi* means, like in *I bi gsi*. I kept hearing that. (In High German this is *Ich bin gewesen*, and in English "I was" or "I have been".)

Jen rarely needs High German. Her husband writes official letters for them and she speaks to her children's teachers in Swiss German and writes to them in English. She would also be able to write in Swiss German if they didn't understand English. She speaks and writes in English for her job in an international company, which means there has never been any pressure to learn High German there. She is satisfied with her decision to learn Swiss German rather than High German and recommends that if people don't need High German for work, then they should do as she did and learn Swiss German. "You feel much more integrated in the society."

As well as the argument from personality, circumstances can be a driver in the decision as to which language to learn. If you are immersed in a situation where everyone around you is speaking Swiss German, it makes sense to turn the constant input you are getting into something meaningful as soon as possible.

Instant integration

Some people speak fluent Swiss German although they have never lived in Switzerland and do not know it very well. Sofia is a primary school teacher in Canton Bern who grew up in Greece. She has Swiss nationality and speaks fluent Swiss German because her mother is Swiss. She speaks a dialect from Biel, which meant that she experienced a kind of "instant integration" although she had only ever been to Switzerland on holiday. "Speaking dialect means you belong," she told me. She was immediately accepted as an insider, although she did not yet feel at home in Switzerland. The only indication that Sofia was different came from the expressions she used. "When I say swear words like *Gopfertori* or *Gopfridstutz*, my colleagues tell me I sound like their grandmother."

Prestige or belonging

Swiss German is very important to local people who speak it. Some Swiss linguists even argue that it has higher prestige than High German. Local people I spoke to think the word "belonging" fits much better to describe the value of dialect. I tried to argue that the sense of belonging amounts to a form of "hidden prestige", as American linguists call it.[43] Dialect appears to be of lower status in society, but is actually of higher status because it allows you to be accepted by an "in-group" of Swiss German speakers.

I found that people were not buying the "prestige" concept, hidden or otherwise. They agreed with my next suggestion that it would be more useful to say that speaking Swiss German is of high *value*. This is a more pragmatic term. Prestige is just about how things look. Dialect has value because it helps you to feel part of things on a deeper level in in your local community. You may be able to belong without it, but it certainly helps to have it.

Dialect-speaking coconuts

Feeling part of things is a clear benefit of learning Swiss German (or Swiss High German with a Swiss accent and a few dialect words thrown in for some local flavour). The sense of belonging can be seen with reference to the peach and coconut model discussed in Chapter 5. Speaking Swiss German can counteract the apparent formality of relationships among strangers on the "outside of the coconut". Nathalie, a Swiss colleague, explained it to me as follows:

> At a job interview, two German-speaking Swiss who do not know each other will speak Swiss German. Although they will use surnames and behave formally, speaking Swiss German will allow them to have a sense of closeness and belonging that they would not have if they were speaking High German. They will not say it, but they will feel it.

It is as if the use of dialect allows people to cut through the outer shell of the coconut and takes them into the private inner layer. They may actually be creating a bond below the surface. If they spoke High German they would feel stiffer and less comfortable and also be concerned about making mistakes.

"*Channinozalla*?" Writing Swiss German

Many incomers are baffled by the sounds they are hearing around them in Swiss German and cannot make sense of them. Some hear the same expression used repeatedly and just parrot chunks of language the way they hear it. Mick, an English colleague, told me that when he lived in Zürich he picked up an expression to use in restaurants. He just said something like *Channinozalla?* (or *Chann i no zalla*, meaning "Can I pay?") and a bill was brought to his table. It was a mystery to him what it actually meant. He did not realise that the verb "can" was in there somewhere.

Nowadays local people mostly write their texts to each other in Swiss German. There is no standard spelling for most dialects, so they can write as they like. This can be a good way to learn, as you see the separate words and have time to study and decipher the message. Moritz is a German student in Basel, and is a member of a hockey club. The team members write to each other about their hockey matches in WhatsApp. Moritz understands almost everything he reads, but does not yet understand as much when the team members talk to each other in Swiss German. If he just hears someone saying *memuessnidinallerherrgottsfriehufsto*, he hasn't a chance of understanding. Once he sees the words all written separately, as shown below, he can work out the meaning:

Marco: Wenn isch d Match? Samstig oder Sunntig?
Luca: Sunntig Monsieur! Und 15:15 in Gänf, d.h. me muess nid in aller herrgottsfrieh ufsto.

(Translation:
Marco: When is the match? Saturday or Sunday?
Luca: Sunday, Monsieur! And 15.15 in Geneva, that means we needn't get up at the crack of dawn.)

The future of dialect

Things are changing in Switzerland and younger people today use High German more than their elders did when they were young. This is partly due to TV and social media (e.g. watching videos on YouTube) and also as a result of speaking High German more at school.[44] Most teachers now insist on pupils speaking High German almost all the time from primary school onward. This is a positive development for learners of High German, as younger people are used to speaking High German all day. They tend to feel comfortable speaking High German to people who are learning it.

Some Swiss people feel concerned that the increase in the use of High German at school means that dialects could die out. It is good to be aware of this concern. Swiss parents, for example, report that their children say *Pferd* instead of *Ross* for a horse, or *Frühstück* instead of *Z'Morge* for breakfast. It is true that dialects are changing, and some dialect words are being replaced by High German words. City dialects are influencing the dialects of smaller towns and villages around them and in this way older words are getting lost too.

These changes are seen as completely natural by linguists and they reassure the population that Swiss German is more popular than ever. Local people have a deep commitment to their Swiss German dialects. As the linguist, Markus Gasser, commented on Radio SRF 1, "Dialect is booming, dialect is cool."[45] He explained that in contrast to Germany, speaking dialect has never been a sign of a lack of education and that it has conquered the new domains of text messages and email.

When I first came to Switzerland I was desperate to see some written Swiss German. Examples of it were few and far between. I see all the messages now being written in dialect as a very useful "corpus" for people who can speak High German and wish to understand the local dialect. They can ask people to write to them in dialect, decipher the messages, and start learning to recognise the dialect words they hear around them.

At the same time, it would be of great benefit to dialect learners if more language schools would offer the option of Swiss German as a language course for beginners with no previous knowledge of High German. This would be an important contribution to the integration of incomers, so that they could more quickly become insiders.

Appendix A

Correct answers to Swiss German quiz on pages 185–186
Section A 1b 2a 3c
Section B 1. False 2. True 3. True 4. False

Notes

1. 63.3% of the population of Switzerland speak German or Swiss German as their main language, 22.7% speak French and 8.1% speak Italian.

2. http://www.newlyswissed.com/more-things-to-known-before-moving-to-switzerland/ by Dimitri Burkhard, 30 December 2016.

3. Geert Hofstede, Gert Jan Hofstede, Michael Minkov (2010). *Cultures and Organisations. Software of the mind.* 3rd Edition, McGraw-Hill, USA.

4. Nick Enfield (2002). *Ethnosyntax: Explorations in grammar and culture.* Oxford University Press.

5. Davoine, E., Schröter, O.C. et Stern, J. (2014). "Cultures régionales des filiales dans l'entreprise multinationale et capacités d'influence liées à la langue: une étude de cas." In *Ancrages culturels et dynamiques du Management International.* Volume 18, Special Issue, 2014.

6. See note 5.

7. TMA Worldprism language of difference. www.countrynavigator.com.

8. Some of the examples in this chapter are taken from: Margaret Oertig (2012). *Going Local – your guide to Swiss schooling.* Bergli Books.

9. Clotaire Rapaille. (2006). *The culture code.* Broadway Books.

10. Franz Eberle und Mitarbeitende (2008). *EVAMAR II Evaluation der Maturitätsreform 1995 (EVAMAR) Phase II.* Universität Zürich, Institut für Gymnasial- und Berufspädagogik.

11. See the original *Beyond Chocolate – understanding Swiss culture* (2002, 2011). Bergli Books, by Margaret Oertig, available as an e-book.

12. The idea is based on a distinction made by Kurt Lewin, a German-American

psychologist, who was interested in the boundaries of the public and private 'life spaces' of Germans and Americans.

13. https://www.bfs.admin.ch/bfs/de/home/statistiken/mobilitaet-verkehr /personenverkehr/pendlermobilitaet.html.

14. Markus Freitag (Ed) (2014). *Das soziale Kapital der Schweiz*. NZZ Libro.

15. Ron Scollon and Suzie Wong Scollon. (1995). *Intercultural Communication*. Blackwell.

16. Thanks to Tony, who first described this ritual verbal exchange as a dance in 2002.

17. https://dima.sbb.ch/unterwegs/artikel/71912/du-was-soll-das-mit -dem-du.

18. Jonathan Strickland. *How road rage works*. https://auto.howstuffworks .com/car-driving-safety/accidents-hazardous-conditions/road-rage4.htm.

19. Valeska Blank. *Machen sich Bosse mit Mittelinitial wichtig?* 20Minuten. ch, 16 February 2017.

20. Silviane Roche. *Bonjour docteur(e). Du bon usage des titres*. Le Temps, 16 June 2012.

21. Phillip Tingler. *Gehört der Doktortitel zum Grüezi?* Migros Magazin, Ausgabe 35, 29 August 2016.

22. See note 8.

23. https://www.beobachter.ch/wohnen/nachbarn/wohnen-kampfzone -balkon.

24. Google "comparis" and "personal legal protection" (in English) to get more information on the different types of cover. Prices range from 130 to 230 CHF per year.

25. https://www.wandern.ch/de/signalisation.

26. Sylvie Chevrier (2009). Is national culture still relevant to management in a global context? The case of Switzerland. *International Journal of Cross-Cultural Management*, Vol. 9, No 2, p169–183.

27. Miryam Eser Davolio and Eva Tov (2009). Deutsche und Schweizer: Gegensätzliche Führungsstile bergen Konflikte. *HR Today* online, 1 May 2009.

28. KPMG Insights. *Unfocused actions won't help.* 5 August 2015. https://home.kpmg.com/ch/en/home/insights/2015/08/interview-hans-ulrich-bigler.html.

29. James MacGregor Burns (2003). *Transforming leadership: A new pursuit of happiness.* New York. Atlantic Monthly Press.

30. PhD by Benjamin Staehleli (2003). *Cross-cultural management within Switzerland: an in-depth case study of a Swiss financial services company.* BS-Verlag Zürich.

31. See note 5.

32. Anna Wierzbicka (1999). *Emotions across languages and cultures. Diversity and universals.* Cambridge: Cambridge University Press. Pages 240–246.

33. Christian Hannig (2006). Interkulturelle Kommunikation im Rettungsdienst. In D. Kumbier & F. Schultz von Thun (Eds.), *Interkulturelle Kommunikation: Methoden, Modelle, Beispiele.*

34. Susan Cain (2012). *Quiet: The power of introverts in a world that can't stop talking.* Crown Publishing Group.

35. Peter Sieber und Horst Sitta (1986). *Mundart und Standardsprache als Problem der Schule.* Aarau: Verlag Sauerländer.

36. The umbrella term "university" is used to refer to traditional universities and universities of applied sciences.

37. See note 8.

38. https://www.fhnw.ch/en/degree-programmes/international/incomings.

39. Allensbacher Archiv, IfD-Umfrage 10016, February 2008.

40. Translation of words: *ig* (ich/ I), *chlii* (klein/ small), *glii* (gleich/soon), *e bitzeli* (ein bisschen/ a little), *Schoggi* (Schokolade/chocolate) and *gell*? (nicht wahr?/isn't it?).

41. Hans Bickel und Christoph Landolt (2012). *Schweizerhochdeutsch. Wörterbuch der Standardsprache in der deutschen Schweiz.* Mannheim und Zürich. Dudenverlag.

42. Martin Müller et al (2009). *Chunsch Druus? Schweizerdeutsch verstehen – Die Deutschschweiz verstehen.* Bern: Schulverlag AG.

43. Walt Wolfram (2004). *Social Varieties of American English.* Cambridge University Press.

44. Schweizerische Konferenz der kantonalen Erziehungsdirektoren (EDK). Beschluss Plenarversammlung, 12. Juni 2003. Aktionsplan «PISA 2000»-Folgemassnahmen, S. 7. (www.edk.ch)

45. *Unsere Dialekte werden nicht aussterben.* Interview with Markus Gasser, Radio SRF 2, 29. April 2015.

Acknowledgments

No writer is an island and this book was very much a joint effort. My thanks go firstly to the team at Bergli Books and my editor, Richard Harvell, for his objectivity balanced with encouragement and support. He had a keen eye for the key themes and without him the book would have gone off at many tangents on cultural values around the world.

I also wish to express my gratitude to Dianne Dicks, my first editor and the founder of Bergli Books. Dianne invited me to speak at a Talk Party on politeness across cultures in the Bider und Tanner bookshop in Basel in 2001. She observed the lively exchange of stories about faux pas in Switzerland among the participants, and this led to her vision for a book explaining Swiss attitudes to politeness to incomers. I was given the task of writing the book. Thanks, Dianne, for your vision, your confidence in me and your patience and guidance over the years.

The New Beyond Chocolate grew out of the themes developed in the original book of 2002. I would like to express my appreciation to all contributors for their openness and generosity as they shared their stories, perspectives and wisdom. It is not possible to quote all the "co-producers of knowledge", but their insights were all very valuable and have strongly influenced the direction of the themes in the new book.

My thanks also go to my family for their support in the writing of this book. My Swiss husband, Hans, was my first teacher on the subject of cultural values in Switzerland and still helps me to understand what may be going on in the minds of local people today when they interact with incomers. Our Swiss daughters, Fiona and Sarah, have both encouraged me and shared their views with me over many years, first as young people, and more recently as adults. They helped me to identify early which aspects of culture are changing most in Switzerland, and I am grateful for their support. I also wish to thank my mother, Betty Davidson, for her continuing interest in my writing, with all its ups and downs.

My understanding of what was going on beneath the surface in my intercultural interactions in Switzerland began many years ago, when Hans and I were newly married. We attended an intercultural couples' discussion group at the home of Dr Jakob Christ and his wife, Jane Christ. There we discussed a range of cultural topics and discovered that some of the British and American wives were arguing with their Swiss husbands about similar, seemingly trivial issues.

One topic was "fitting in" and whether the Swiss husbands should worry about what Swiss people thought, for example, if their foreign wives wanted to put up their Christmas trees in early December instead of on Christmas Eve. I am grateful to Jake and Jane for having given us this unique opportunity to start discussing our cultural values with others.

What started as an exploration of values in my private life ended up becoming a theme in my working life and as a writer too. I hope that the values expressed through the stories in this book will give you food for thought as you explore and discuss your own cultural values and those of the people around you.

Index

U

Unfocused action, 131
University (*See* Studying in
    Switzerland)

V

Verb forms, 21
Village life
    joining local activities, 86
    knowing everyone else's business,
        86
    Mittagstisch, 86
    openness to change, 85–86
    political autonomy, 87–88
    village party for whole village
        (Dorffest), 92

W

Waiting tables in restaurants,
    144–145
Walking paths, 111–112
Wedding ceremony metaphor, 122
White space on advertisements, 76
Whitwill, Theo, 178
Wierzbicka, Anna, 149

Wine drinking, 74–75
Work environment
    celebrating success, 46
    coffee break, 43
    deadlines, 136, 141–142
    decision making (*See* Decision
        making)
    flexitime, 31
    impression management, 32–33
    keeping appointments, 145–146
    last minute requests, 139–140
    lunch, 42
    mistakes and their consequences,
        137–138
    networking, 43, 166
    planning, 23–25
    praise, 157–158
    project management, 108–109
    punctuality, 31–32
    reflect, analyse, prepare, 131
    socialising outside of work,
        44–47
    surprises, 121
    taking up space (*See* Taking up
        space at work)
    task-force mode, 142–143